GRADE **5**

Word Analysis Workbook

SAVVAS
LEARNING COMPANY

ISBN-13: 978-0-328-96306-5
ISBN-10: 0-328-96306-2

12 22

Contents

Spelling

Name _____

Short Vowel VCCV, VCV

Spelling Words				
distance	method	anger	problem	butter
petals	enjoy	perhaps	figure	channel
admire	comedy	husband	tissue	mustard
shuttle	advance	drummer	regular	denim

Words in Context Complete each sentence with a list word.

1. The ____ keeps the rhythm of the band.

2. Most people ____ the skills of talented artists.

3. Watching a ____ makes people laugh.

4. The ____ bus is the fastest way to get there.

5. I like ____ on my hot dog.

6. Her ____ was forty years old.

7. The shortest ____ between two points is a straight line.

8. The ____ fell off the flower one by one.

9. ____ we can have ice cream after dinner.

10. The skater practiced ____ eights on the ice.

1. _____

2. _____

3. _____

4. _____

5. _____

6. _____

7. _____

8. _____

9. _____

10. _____

Word Meanings Write the list word that has nearly the same meaning.

11. handkerchief   11. _____

12. canal   12. _____

13. lard   13. _____

14. technique   14. _____

15. like   15. _____

16. proceed   16. _____

17. rage   17. _____

18. jeans   18. _____

19. usual   19. _____

20. difficulty   20. _____

Home Activity Your child wrote words that have short vowels. Dictate words and have your child say and spell each word.

1

Name _____

Short Vowel VCCV, VCV

Proofread a Poster Sarah made a poster for the school fair. Circle seven spelling errors. Find one capitalization error. Write the corrections on the lines.

> Come too the village fair!
>
> See the funny comady team show.
>
> Milk a cow and churn some buttar at the farm exhibit.
>
> Sample hot dogs with twenty choices of musterd!
>
> Make tisseu flower bouquets.
>
> Decorate your denim jeans with a special new art method.
>
> Enjoy fifty booths of crafts, fun, and games.
>
> park at the Town Hall parking lot.
>
> Ride the special shuttal bus to the fairgrounds.
>
> Discount tickets are on sale in advanse.

Spelling Words

distance
method
anger
problem
butter
petals
enjoy
perhaps
figure
channel

admire
comedy
husband
tissue
mustard
shuttle
advance
drummer
regular
denim

1. _____   2. _____

3. _____   4. _____

5. _____   6. _____

7. _____

8. _____

Frequently Misspelled Words

and
to
too

Proofread Words Circle the correct spelling of the word.

9. channal   chanel   channel

10. drummer   drumer   drummor

11. metod   methid   method

12. parhaps   perhaps   pirhaps

13. figure   figger   figour

14. petles   petels   petals

15. problam   problem   problim

Home Activity Your child found misspelled list words with VCCV and VCV patterns. Select a list word and ask your child to spell it.

Name _____

Long Vowel VCV

Spelling Words

fever	broken	climate	hotel	basic
vocal	native	silent	labor	spider
label	icon	agent	motive	vital
acorn	item	aroma	ego	solo

Words in Context Complete each sentence with a list word.

1. From a small ____, a large oak tree grows.   1. _____

2. When you are sick, you may have a ____.   2. _____

3. Your ____ is what you think of yourself.   3. _____

4. Flying ____ means doing something alone.   4. _____

5. A desert ____ may produce too little rain to support crops.   5. _____

6. The two people were loud and ____ as they cheered.   6. _____

7. The travel ____ helped plan a vacation.   7. _____

8. We want to stay in the ____ that has a pool.   8. _____

9. Have you ever watched a ____ spin its web?   9. _____

10. The clothing ____ itches the back of my neck.   10. _____

Antonyms Write the list word that has the opposite or nearly the opposite meaning.

11. fixed   11. _____

12. advanced   12. _____

13. alien   13. _____

14. noisy   14. _____

15. unimportant   15. _____

Synonyms Write the list word that has the same or nearly the same meaning.

16. work   16. _____

17. reason   17. _____

18. object   18. _____

19. scent   19. _____

20. image   20. _____

Home Activity Your child wrote words with the long vowel VCV pattern. Have your child tell you one synonym or one antonym for a list word.

Name _____

Long Vowel VCV

Proofread a Postcard Yolanda wrote a postcard to her friend. Circle six spelling errors and one capitalization error. Write the corrections on the lines.

> dear Margaret,
>
>   I'm having a great time at the hotle. There are lemon trees everywhere and the eroma from the blossoms is awesome. Today, I'm going to by some gifts. There are many nateve crafts to choose from. It's very calm and silant here. The only noise comes from the wind and the ocean. Thank your travel agant for suggesting this place. It's now a family favorite!
>
>   Your friend,
>   Yolanda

Spelling Words
fever
broken
climate
hotel
basic
vocal
native
silent
labor
spider
label
icon
agent
motive
vital
acorn
item
aroma
ego
solo

1. _____ 2. _____

3. _____ 4. _____

5. _____ 6. _____

7. _____

Proofread Words Circle the correct spelling of the word.

8.	vocle	vocal	vocel
9.	label	laebel	labal
10.	brokin	brokan	broken
11.	basec	basic	basuc
12.	ikon	icon	ican
13.	motive	motife	motove
14.	akorn	acern	acorn
15.	fever	fevar	feaver
16.	eego	ego	egho

Frequently Misspelled Words
favorite
buy

Home Activity Your child identified misspelled list words in a paragraph. Ask your child to name one list word with the long *a* sound and one with the long *o* sound.

4

Name _____

Long Vowel Digraphs

Words in Context Complete each sentence with a list word.

1. I am dizzy and may ____.   1. _____

2. A perfect ____ score is 300.   2. _____

3. I had multi-____ bread in my sandwich.   3. _____

4. High ____ tells you that you did a great job.   4. _____

5. Make a ____ in the paper to fold it in half.   5. _____

6. Food grilled over a ____ fire tastes great.   6. _____

7. It is generally better to be positive than to ____.   7. _____

8. A sailboat needs a strong ____ to go fast.   8. _____

9. Antique car owners spend time and money to ____ their   9. _____
   vehicles so they will continue to run.

10. Two countries that border ____ are Portugal and France.   10. _____

Classifying Write the list word that belongs in each group.

11. bow, feather, ____   11. _____

12. sew, thread, ____   12. _____

13. glide, cruise, ____   13. _____

14. cold, cough, ____   14. _____

15. corn, barley, ____   15. _____

16. talk, lecture, ____   16. _____

Synonyms Write the list word that has the same or nearly the same meaning.

17. request   17. _____   18. banquet   18. _____

19. tree   19. _____   20. color   20. _____

Home Activity Your child wrote words with long vowel digraphs. Have your child tell you two ways to spell long *e*.

5

Long Vowel Digraphs

Proofread a Report Miguel wrote about his family's trip. Circle six spelling errors. Find one punctuation error. Write the corrections on the lines.

Spelling Words

coast
feast
speech
wheat
Spain
paint
arrow
needle
charcoal
praise

faint
maintain
crease
grain
breeze
willow
appeal
bowling
complain
sneeze

    This summer, my family traveled to Spain. We felt very lucky to stay in a hotel right on the caost. The weather was always beautiful with a light breaze blowing in off the ocean. Outside my window, the branches of a wilow tree dipped into a small pond. The sky was the same color as the baby blue color in my pante box. On our last night we had a wonderful feest. I thought I would fante at the sight of so much food! Everything was really delicious? My stomach hurt before we got to dessert. Is that anything to complain about?

1. _____   2. _____

3. _____   4. _____

5. _____   6. _____

7. _____

Frequently
Misspelled
Words

Halloween
really

Proofread Words Circle the correct spelling of the word.

8. weat   wheet   wheat

9. charcole   charcoal   charcol

10. maintain   maintane   mantain

11. boling   bolling   bowling

12. complain   complane   complan

13. creese   creaze   crease

14. arow   arrow   arro

Home Activity Your child corrected misspelled list words in a paragraph and selected the correctly spelled word in a group of words. Select three list words and ask your child to spell them.

Name _____

Adding -ed, -ing

Word Pairs Write the best list words to complete each sentence pair.

Were you (1)_____ with lunch? I found the food very (2)_____.

1. _____   2. _____

David (3)_____ that he lost his key. (4)_____ guilt was the best thing to do in his case.

3. _____   4. _____

Did you see the eclipse as it was (5)_____? Last time one (6)_____, I missed it.

5. _____   6. _____

The runners lined up for the (7)_____ race. After that race, only three runners (8)_____ for the team.

7. _____   8. _____

My lost cat has an (9)_____ number tattooed on her skin. She was easily (10)_____ as mine when she was found.

9. _____   10. _____

I have so much trouble (11)_____ between piano or karate lessons. Have you (12)_____ on a choice yet?

11. _____   12. _____

The coach used many (13)_____ tactics, such as time-outs, during the game. Then the final quarter was (14)_____ by the rain.

13. _____   14. _____

The school closet was fully (15)_____ with pencils. Do you think the school will be (16)_____ pencils for the big test?

15. _____   16. _____

Stop (17)_____ that you broke the window! Even though you (18)_____ it, we all saw your ball break the window.

17. _____   18. _____

Are you (19)_____ olives on your shopping list? I've (20)_____ carrots, celery, and pickles on my list.

19. _____   20. _____

Home Activity Your child wrote words with -ed and -ing endings. Select a list word and ask your child to tell you its meaning.

7

Name _____

Adding -ed, -ing

Proofread a Newspaper Article This is an article from a local weekly newspaper. Circle six spelling errors. Write the sentence with a punctuation error correctly. Write the corrections on the lines below.

Adding -ed, -ing

Three Caught After Holdup
by Rosy Redeye

   The crime ocurred after midnight. The store's videotape identifyed three suspects. The store owner supplyed the license plate number to the police department. Geting the results took no time. The police quickly located the car and suspects They had trouble admiting their wrongdoing. However, in front of the judge, they deceided to admit everything. The police were satisfied that they had solved the case.

---

1. _____   2. _____

3. _____   4. _____

5. _____   6. _____

7. _____

Proofread Words Circle the correct spelling of the word.

8. occured	occurred	ocured
9. included	includid	includ
10. qualifed	qualifide	qualified
11. deceided	decided	decieded
12. satesfying	satisfying	satisfiying
13. admitted	admited	admetted
14. suppliing	sapplying	supplying

Spelling Words

supplied
supplying
denied
denying
decided
deciding
included
including
admitted
admitting

occurred
occurring
qualified
qualifying
identified
identifying
delayed
delaying
satisfied
satisfying

Frequently Misspelled Words

getting
decided
stopped

Home Activity Your child identified misspelled list words. Select three list words and ask your child to spell them.

Name _____

Contractions

Spelling Words				
they're	you've	weren't	needn't	there'd
they've	mustn't	what'll	doesn't	hadn't
could've	would've	should've	might've	wouldn't
who've	shouldn't	who'd	this'll	couldn't

Contractions Write the contraction that can be made from the underlined words.

1. <u>They are</u> going on a school trip to the museum.   1. _____

2. The students <u>need not</u> bring lunch because the museum has a cafeteria.   2. _____

3. <u>This will</u> be an educational and fun trip.   3. _____

4. Students <u>must not</u> bring umbrellas or backpacks.   4. _____

5. Those <u>who have</u> taken the tour can go to the bookstore.   5. _____

6. Those <u>who would</u> rather not go, please report to Room 303.   6. _____

7. Students <u>should not</u> talk during the tour.   7. _____

8. We <u>could not</u> hear the tour guide.   8. _____

9. Anyone who <u>does not</u> behave will not be allowed to go on
   the next trip.   9. _____

10. Students <u>would not</u> want to disappoint their teacher.   10. _____

Questions Write the contraction that completes each answer.

11. Do they have any ice cream at the stand? No, _____ sold out.   11. _____

12. Would they have eaten popcorn instead? Yes, they _____.   12. _____

13. Should I have thrown the ball? Yes, you _____.   13. _____

14. Could I have handed in my project yesterday? Yes, you _____.   14. _____

15. Had the students worn these coats before? No, they _____.   15. _____

16. Would there be another party? Yes, _____ be another party at
    a later date.   16. _____

17. Might they have joined in the fun? They _____, but they had to go home. 17. _____

18. Do you know what will happen tomorrow? No one knows _____ happen
    tomorrow.   18. _____

19. Were the boys at the game? No, they _____ there.   19. _____

20. Do you have my book? No, _____ put it in your locker.   20. _____

School + Home **Home Activity** Your child wrote contractions. Say two words and have your child combine them into a contraction and spell the word.

9

Name _____

Contractions

Proofread a Conversation Jack wrote this conversation between a waiter and a diner. Circle six spelling errors and one punctuation error. Write the corrections on the lines.

> "Whatll you have for lunch?" asked the waiter.
> "I'm not sure," said the diner.
> "Maybe this'll tempt you—lima bean casserole!" said the waiter.
> "Who'ud eat that for lunch?" asked the diner.
> "That's a very popular dish around here," said the waiter.
> "Theyr'e already lining up outside the door for the beans."
> "You were'nt kidding about a long line," said the diner.
> You mustn't miss this tasty treat," said the waiter.
> "Okay, I wouldn't want to miss your special dish!" said the diner. "Hey, this doesnt taste too bad at all!"
> "See what you would've been missing if you had'nt tried our special dish!" said the waiter.

1. _____   2. _____

3. _____   4. _____

5. _____   6. _____

7. _____

_____

Proofread Words Circle the correct spelling of the word.

8. wood've	woud've	would've
9. dosn't	doesn't	dosen't
10. weren't	wearn't	wheren't
11. coudn't	culdn't	couldn't
12. might've	mihgt've	mitgth've
13. whatll	whatl'l	what'll
14. who'd	who'ld	whod'd

Spelling Words

they're
you've
weren't
needn't
there'd
they've
mustn't
what'll
doesn't
hadn't

could've
would've
should've
might've
wouldn't
who've
shouldn't
who'd
this'll
couldn't

Frequently Misspelled Words

that's
you're
doesn't

School + Home

Home Activity Your child identified misspelled list words. Select contractions and ask your child to tell you how they were formed.

Name _____

Short Vowel VCCV, VCV

Alphabetize Write the twelve list words below in alphabetical order.

method	comedy
denim	anger
distance	enjoy
perhaps	advance
admire	figure
channel	regular

1. _____
2. _____
3. _____
4. _____
5. _____
6. _____

7. _____
8. _____
9. _____
10. _____
11. _____
12. _____

Hidden Words Each of these small words can be found inside one of the list words. Write the list word that contains the small word.

13. sue _____
14. rob _____
15. drum _____
16. pet _____

17. ban _____
18. shut _____
19. but _____
20. tar _____

School + Home

Home Activity Your child learned to spell longer words with short vowel sounds. Find words with short vowel sounds in a magazine or newspaper and ask your child to spell them.

Long Vowel VCV

Spelling Words				
fever	broken	climate	hotel	basic
vocal	native	silent	labor	spider
label	icon	agent	motive	vital
acorn	item	aroma	ego	solo

Analogies Write the word that completes each comparison.

1. Mouth is to taste as nose is to _____.

2. Loud is to deafening as quiet is to _____.

3. Cold is to chill as hot is to _____.

4. Robin is to bird as black widow is to _____.

5. Two is to duet as one is to _____.

6. Cottage is to house as inn is to _____.

7. Vine is to grape as oak tree is to _____.

8. Smart is to intelligent as self-esteem is to _____.

9. Friend is to enemy as stranger is to _____.

10. Sleep is to rest as work is to _____.

Word Clues Write the list word that fits each clue.

11. This includes a place's temperatures and rainfall. _____

12. You'll find one of these sewn into a piece of clothing. _____

13. You can't use something described as this. _____

14. An actor or athlete might employ this person. _____

15. A person who speaks up is described this way. _____

16. This explains why you did something. _____

17. This describes something that is absolutely necessary. _____

18. You can click on one of these on a Web site. _____

19. This is another word for a thingamajig. _____

20. This describes something that is not advanced. _____

School + Home

Home Activity Your child learned to spell longer words with long vowel sounds. To practice at home, make up clues about words with long vowel sounds and ask your child to spell them.

Name _____

Long Vowel Digraphs

Spelling Words				
coast	feast	speech	wheat	Spain
paint	arrow	needle	charcoal	praise
faint	maintain	crease	grain	breeze
willow	appeal	bowling	complain	sneeze

Word Search Circle ten hidden list words. Words are down, across, and diagonal.
Write the words on the lines.

```
F  B  W  S  P  P  A  D  E  Y
N  J  O  I  C  F  A  I  N  T
A  L  A  W  E  R  B  I  P  O
G  Q  W  I  L  L  O  W  N  M
R  T  U  A  E  I  S  U  G  T
A  E  S  P  A  I  N  N  W  Y
I  B  N  P  S  E  G  F  T
N  W  H  E  A  T  E  N  O  P
E  K  S  A  I  k  Z  E  N  l
H  E  E  L  C  R  E  A  S  E
```

1. _____   6. _____

2. _____   7. _____

3. _____   8. _____

4. _____   9. _____

5. _____   10. _____

Scramble Unscramble the list words and write them on the lines.

11. elende _____   16. timinana _____

12. worar _____   17. shepec _____

13. sarpie _____   18. larhocca _____

14. zerbee _____   19. stafe _____

15. ascto _____   20. aclimpon _____

Home Activity Your child learned to spell words with long vowel digraphs. Ask your child to give examples of and spell words with *ea, ee, ai, oa,* and *ow.*

Adding -ed, -ing

Spelling Words				
supplied	supplying	denied	denying	decided
deciding	included	including	admitted	admitting
occurred	occurring	qualified	qualifying	identified
identifying	delayed	delaying	satisfied	satisfying

Antonyms Write the list word ending in -ed that has the opposite or nearly the opposite meaning.

1. unhappy _____

2. on time _____

3. denied _____

4. excluded _____

5. unsure _____

Synonyms Write the list word ending in -ed that has the same or nearly the same meaning.

6. happened _____

7. named _____

8. furnished _____

9. confessed _____

10. able; competent _____

Word Clues Write the list word that fits each clue.

11. what a lawbreaker is doing to avoid getting in trouble _____

12. what an athlete is doing in a regional track meet _____

13. what trucks full of food are doing at the supermarket _____

14. what a jury is doing after a trial _____

15. what an event is doing while it is underway _____

16. what a detective is attempting by looking at fingerprints _____

17. what a school is doing when it lets students in _____

18. what an airline is doing to passengers when running late _____

19. what a delicious meal is doing for your hunger _____

20. what you are doing when you put everything in _____

Home Activity Your child learned to spell words with -ed and -ing. To practice at home, name three verbs that describe after-school activities. Ask your child to spell each word with an -ed ending and with an -ing ending.

Name _____

Contractions

Spelling Words				
they're	you've	weren't	needn't	there'd
they've	mustn't	what'll	doesn't	hadn't
could've	would've	should've	might've	wouldn't
who've	shouldn't	who'd	this'll	couldn't

Words in Context Complete each sentence with a list word.

1. The students want to raise money, so _____ selling fruit.

2. James had been to big cities, but he _____ ever been to Chicago.

3. I had never met anyone _____ been to Africa.

4. The electricity is out, so _____ we do about dinner?

5. We have practiced for weeks, so _____ be the best school play ever.

6. We'll go to the zoo after lunch since it _____ open until noon on Monday.

7. Several players _____ at the first soccer practice.

8. If there were a big storm, _____ be many people without food and water.

9. You may help chop vegetables, but you _____ cut yourself.

10. It's raining; I knew I _____ brought my umbrella.

11. I just realized I _____ left my spelling book at home.

12. You need to bring a pillow to camp, but you _____ bring a sleeping bag.

13. _____ you like to go swimming?

14. Sophia tried, but she _____ open the jar.

15. The Scotts aren't home; _____ gone to Florida for two weeks.

16. It may rain Saturday, but it _____ affect our plans.

17. Put the dressing on the salad after _____ mixed it well.

18. If I _____ found my cap, I would've worn it to the game.

19. I admire people _____ climbed high mountains.

20. Our team _____ won the game if we'd gotten one more goal.

Home Activity Your child learned to spell contractions. Ask your child to give examples of and spell contractions formed with the words *are*, *not*, *have*, and *will*.

Digraphs *th*, *sh*, *ch*, *ph*

Spelling Words				
shovel	southern	northern	chapter	hyphen
chosen	establish	although	challenge	approach
astonish	python	shatter	ethnic	shiver
pharmacy	charity	china	attach	ostrich

Word Meanings Write the list word that has the same or nearly the meaning as the underlined words.

1. We are raising money for a <u>worthy cause</u>.

2. The <u>drugstore</u> filled the prescription for the medicine.

3. The United States is made up of many people from different <u>cultural</u> groups.

4. The restaurant chain wants to <u>set up</u> a diner in the community.

5. We set the table with our best <u>glass dishes</u>.

6. The best way to succeed is to constantly <u>test</u> yourself.

7. The cool breeze sent a <u>quiver</u> down my back.

8. I never would have <u>selected</u> those blue jackets.

9. The plane was on its final <u>move</u> toward the runway.

10. The magic trick was crafted to <u>amaze</u> the unsuspecting audience.

1. _____

2. _____

3. _____

4. _____

5. _____

6. _____

7. _____

8. _____

9. _____

10. _____

Classifying Write the list word that belongs in each group.

11. even if, while, ___

12. cobra, rattler, ___

13. fasten, join, ___

14. spade, scoop, ___

15. episode, part, ___

16. smash, break, ___

17. peacock, swan, ___

18. dash, line, ___

11. _____

12. _____

13. _____

14. _____

15. _____

16. _____

17. _____

18. _____

Home Activity Your child matched list words with synonyms. Name two list words and see if your child can give a synonym for each.

Name _____

Digraphs *th*, *sh*, *ch*, *ph*

Proofread a Poster Circle five spelling errors. Find one sentence with a punctuation error. Write the corrections on the lines.

> Come to the charaty auction for the
> new recreation center.
>
> Help dig the building site. Buy a chance to
> shovle some earth.
>
> Bid on and buy, wonderful prizes from around the world!
>
> Challange yourself in contests and games.
>
> Bid on lovely china figures and platters.
>
> Sample delicious northurn and southern cooking!
>
> Time: Saturday, from 9 A.M. to 6 P.M.
>
> Place: The old pharmecy building

1. _____   2. _____

3. _____   4. _____

5. _____

6. _____

_____

Proofread Words Circle the correct spelling of the word.

7. The ending of the book will ____ you.
   astonish   astonesh   astonash

8. I need a stapler to ____ the poster to the bulletin board.
   attatch   attach   atach

9. Music is my ____ field of study.
   chosen   chozen   choicen

10. I want to read a ____ a day.
    chaptar   shapter   chapter

11. Numbers, such as sixty-five, are written with a ____.
    hiphen   hyphen   hipfen

12. The ____ in the zoo was 12 feet long.
    pythn   python   pithon

Spelling Words

shovel
southern
northern
chapter
hyphen
chosen
establish
although
challenge
approach

astonish
python
shatter
ethnic
shiver
pharmacy
charity
china
attach
ostrich

Home Activity Your child identified misspelled list words. Select words with two different digraph sounds and ask your child to spell them.

Name _____

Irregular Plurals

Words in Context Write a list word to complete each sentence.

1. When people get sick with ____, they get red spots all over their bodies.

2. The ____ of many people's voices bounced around the canyon walls.

3. At the assembly today, two people played ____ for the students.

4. Do you like fresh ____ in your salad?

5. The ____ were caught red-handed with the loot.

6. The old ____ were sagging under the weight of the books.

7. It took eight different ____ to prepare the huge banquet.

8. When ____ erupt, clouds of ash can travel many miles.

9. These ____ are made with waterproof material.

10. We have ____ for everyone who needs to cut ribbons.

1. _____
2. _____
3. _____
4. _____
5. _____
6. _____
7. _____
8. _____
9. _____
10. _____

Classifying Write the list word that belongs in each group.

11. deputies, detectives, ___
12. checkers, chess, ___
13. values, opinions, ___
14. cranes, herons, ___
15. deer, cattle, ___
16. employees, workers, ___
17. breads, buns, ___
18. us, we, ___
19. leaders, bosses, ___
20. tests, examinations, ___

11. _____
12. _____
13. _____
14. _____
15. _____
16. _____
17. _____
18. _____
19. _____
20. _____

Home Activity Your child wrote list words that are irregular plurals to complete sentences and word groups. Name two list words and ask your child to use each in a sentence.

Irregular Plurals

Proofread a List Circle six spelling errors and one capitalization error. Write the corrections on the lines.

Spelling Words

> six scissors
>
> three sets of metal shelfes
>
> twenty sets of dominos
>
> ten waterproof pants
>
> one dozen avacadoes
>
> three toy pianos
>
> twenty-five loavs of bread
>
> three pink Lawn flamingoes

Spelling Words

staffs
ourselves
pants
scissors
loaves
volcanoes
chiefs
buffaloes
flamingos
beliefs

echoes
shelves
quizzes
sheriffs
dominoes
thieves
measles
avocados
chefs
pianos

1. _____   2. _____

3. _____   4. _____

5. _____   6. _____

7. _____

Proofread Words Circle the correct spelling of the word.

8. Almost everyone used to get _____ as a child.

   meesles   measels   measles

9. We had pop _____ in math and science today.

   quizes   quizzes   quizzez

10. People are entitled to their own _____.

    beliefs   believes   beleifs

11. We have no one to blame except _____.

    ourselfs   hourselves   ourselves

12. The music school has three _____ for students to use.

    pianos   pianoes   painos

Frequently Misspelled Words

know
knew

School + Home

Home Activity Your child identified misspelled list words. Select three words from the list and ask your child to spell them to you.

Name _____

Vowel Sounds with *r*

Spelling Words				
snore	tornado	spare	appear	career
square	report	prepare	pioneer	chair
beware	smear	repair	sword	ignore
order	engineer	resort	volunteer	declare

Words in Context Write the list word to complete each sentence.

1. I _____ loudly when I sleep.

2. Have you heard the saying "The pen is mightier than the _____"?

3. The _____ fixed the machine.

4. It was hard to _____ the loud sirens outside.

5. The mayor will _____ a holiday.

6. I have to bring my worn shoes to the shop for _____.

7. We have guests staying in our _____ bedroom.

8. A triangle has three sides; a _____ has four sides.

9. The father told his small child to _____ of traffic.

10. Did the weather _____ forecast rain?

1. _____

2. _____

3. _____

4. _____

5. _____

6. _____

7. _____

8. _____

9. _____

10. _____

Word Groups Write the list word that best completes the group.

11. cyclone, twister, ___

12. show up, materialize, ___

13. job, employment, ___

14. lead the way, be the first, ___

15. get ready, make, ___

16. offer, give aid, ___

17. ask for, send for, ___

18. blur, spread, ___

19. vacation spot, dude ranch, ___

20. seat, bench, ___

11. _____

12. _____

13. _____

14. _____

15. _____

16. _____

17. _____

18. _____

19. _____

20. _____

Home Activity Your child wrote list words that have vowel sounds with *r*. Select three words and ask your child what they mean.

Name _____

Vowel Sounds with *r*

Proofread a Story Ramon wrote this story about sharing a room with his brother. Circle six spelling errors. Find one sentence with a punctuation error. Write the corrections on the lines.

Spelling Words

snore
tornado
spare
appear
career
square
report
prepare
pioneer
chair

beware
smear
repair
sword
ignore
order
engineer
resort
volunteer
declare

My Brother

Mom asked my brother and me to voluntier to give up our rooms for our visiting grandparents. So, we're sharing the spair attic room, but it's no fun. My brother snores, and it's hard to ignoure it. Just as I was falling asleep, he snored like a tornadoe. That was it I threw my pillow at him. It knocked over the lamp, which hit the chare with a loud pop. This did not apear to disturb him at all. I gave up and slept in the hallway as a last resort.

1. _____   2. _____

3. _____   4. _____

5. _____   6. _____

7. _____

Proofread Words Circle the correct spelling of the word.

8. A ____ is someone who leads the way for others.

   pioneer   pioner   pieneer

9. The knight wore a brightly polished ____ on his hip.

   swoard   sword   sworde

10. The ____ is a wind funnel.

   tornado   tornardo   tornadoe

11. Be careful or you'll ____ the fresh paint.

   smear   smere   smeer

12. I asked the bike shop to ____ my flat tire.

   ripare   repair   repare

Frequently Misspelled Words

caught
there's

Home Activity Your child identified misspelled list words in a paragraph. Ask your child to tell you the six patterns used in the list words to spell vowel sounds with *r*.

Name _____

Final Syllables -en, -an, -el, -le, -il

Spelling Words				
example	level	slogan	quarrel	scramble
evil	oxygen	wooden	double	travel
cancel	chuckle	fossil	toboggan	veteran
chisel	suburban	single	sudden	beagle

Word Clues Write the list word that matches each clue.

1. a kind of laugh

2. not urban or rural

3. a kind of sled

4. a gas we breathe

5. something made of oak or maple

6. something that has been preserved in stone

7. a small argument

8. two of something

9. only one

10. a kind of hound dog

1. _____

2. _____

3. _____

4. _____

5. _____

6. _____

7. _____

8. _____

9. _____

10. _____

Synonyms Write a list word that has the same meaning as the underlined word.

11. I found a perfect <u>model</u> of my favorite color.

12. Did you <u>mix</u> the eggs for me?

13. The sculptor had to carefully <u>carve</u> the marble bit by bit.

14. One of my goals is to <u>journey</u> around the world.

15. The ground was <u>flat</u> and then it dropped down steeply.

16. The <u>wicked</u> queen tried to poison her enemy.

17. The company's <u>motto</u> was "Right every time!"

18. The politician was <u>an old hand</u> at running elections.

19. I had to <u>call off</u> my dentist appointment today.

20. The storm was <u>swift</u> and unexpected.

11. _____

12. _____

13. _____

14. _____

15. _____

16. _____

17. _____

18. _____

19. _____

20. _____

Home Activity Your child matched list words to meanings. Ask your child to tell you the meanings of three list words.

Name _____

Final Syllables *-en, -an, -el, -le, -il*

Proofread a Story Sally wrote this story. There are seven spelling errors and one punctuation error. Circle the errors and write the corrections on the lines.

Spelling Words

example
level
slogan
quarrel
scramble
evil
oxygen
wooden
double
travel

cancel
chuckle
fossil
toboggan
veteran
chisel
suburban
single
sudden
beagle

The Old Woodcarver

We decided to travle to see a veteren woodcarver. My dad wanted him to make a tobaggan like the one Dad owned when he was a child. We drove down a long suburben road. When we got out of the car, a beagel ran from behind the house, followed by the woodcarver. He carried an example of a tiny sled made of metal. "Don't worry," he said with a chuckle, "your sled will be wooden." He pulled a chisle out of his pocket. "Would you like to learn how to carve?" he asked. "I may seem like an old fossel to you," he said. "I'm probably double your father's age, but I'm pretty handy with a chisel."

"Sure," I said, "that's a great idea!

1. _____   2. _____

3. _____   4. _____

5. _____   6. _____

7. _____

8. _____

Frequently Misspelled Words

Mom
Dad's
heard

Proofread Words Circle the correct spelling of the word.

9. oxygin	oxygan	oxygen
10. cancel	cancle	cancil
11. quarril	quarrel	quarele
12. evile	eval	evil
13. slogan	slogen	slogin
14. chukle	chuckle	chuckel
15. suddin	suddan	sudden
16. egsample	example	exsampel

Home Activity Your child identified misspelled words with the final syllables *-en, -an, -el, -le,* and *-il.* Ask your child which words are the most difficult for him or her to spell. Have your child spell them.

23

Name _____

Final Syllables -*er*, -*ar*, -*or*

Spelling Words				
danger	wander	tractor	dollar	harbor
eager	eraser	surrender	solar	sticker
locker	helicopter	pillar	refrigerator	caterpillar
rumor	glimmer	linger	sensor	alligator

Definitions Write a list word that means the same or almost the same as the word or phrase.

1. spark

2. port

3. sun

4. gossip

5. post

6. peril

7. cooler

8. excited

9. 100 cents

10. roam

1. _____

2. _____

3. _____

4. _____

5. _____

6. _____

7. _____

8. _____

9. _____

10. _____

Missing Words Write the list word that completes the sentence.

11. I have a habit of chewing on my pencil ____.

12. Smart criminals ____ when spotted.

13. The farmer drove the ____ across the field.

14. I store my schoolbooks in my ____.

15. The ____ floated silently across the swampy water.

16. The ____ became a beautiful butterfly.

17. She pulled the price ____ off the package.

18. The news ____ flew over the accident scene.

19. I like to ____ in my room instead of watching television downstairs.

20. The motion ____ turns on the light when anyone is near.

11. _____

12. _____

13. _____

14. _____

15. _____

16. _____

17. _____

18. _____

19. _____

20. _____

Home Activity Your child wrote words with the final syllables -*er*, -*ar*, and -*or*. Select three list words and ask your child to define them.

Name _____

Final Syllables -*er*, -*ar*, -*or*

Proofread a Sign There are seven spelling errors and one capitalization error. Circle the errors and write the corrections on the lines.

> welcome to the Wildlife and Alligater Preserve
>
> • Admission is one dollar for an all-day parking pass.
> • You can rent an all-day locker for your convenience.
> • Helicoptor rides are available to see the harber from the air.
> • To preserve the ecology, stay on the path.
>   Do not wandar off.
> • There is no dangor. Animals stay behind a motion senser fence.
> • Linger over lunch on our beautiful terrace.
> • Do not forget to surrendar your parking pass at the gate when leaving.

Spelling Words
danger
wander
tractor
dollar
harbor
eager
eraser
surrender
solar
sticker
locker
helicopter
pillar
refrigerator
caterpillar
rumor
glimmer
linger
sensor
alligator

1. _____   2. _____

3. _____   4. _____

5. _____   6. _____

7. _____   8. _____

Frequently Misspelled Words
another
we're

Proofread Words Circle the word that is spelled correctly.

9. doller   dollar   dollor

10. erasor   eraser   erasar

11. stickar   sticker   stickor

12. soler   solar   solor

13. helicoptor   helicoptar   helicopter

14. tracter   tractar   tractor

15. rumer   rumor   rumar

Home Activity Your child identified misspelled words with the final syllables -*er*, -*ar*, and -*or*. Select three list words and ask your child to spell them.

Name _____

Digraphs *th*, *sh*, *ch*, *ph*

Spelling Words				
shovel	hyphen	challenge	shatter	charity
southern	chosen	approach	ethnic	china
northern	establish	astonish	shiver	attach
chapter	although	python	pharmacy	ostrich

Alphabetize Write the ten list words below in alphabetical order.

ethnic	python
ostrich	charity
hyphen	although
chapter	establish
northern	southern

1. _____

2. _____

3. _____

4. _____

5. _____

6. _____

7. _____

8. _____

9. _____

10. _____

Synonyms Write the list word that has the same or nearly the same meaning.

11. surprise _____

12. dare _____

13. shake _____

14. pottery _____

15. picked _____

16. drugstore _____

17. break _____

18. fasten _____

19. dig _____

20. near _____

Home Activity Your child learned to spell words with the digraphs *th*, *sh*, *ch*, and *ph*. Ask your child to give an example of a word with each digraph and spell it.

Irregular Plurals

Spelling Words

staffs	ourselves	pants	scissors	loaves
volcanoes	chiefs	buffaloes	flamingos	beliefs
echoes	shelves	quizzes	sheriffs	dominoes
thieves	measles	avocados	chefs	pianos

Analogies Write the word that completes each comparison.

1. Doctors are to hospitals as _____ are to restaurants.

2. Arms are to shirts as legs are to _____.

3. Drawers are to chests as _____ are to closets.

4. Articles are to essays as tests are to _____.

5. Storm is to tornado as disease is to _____.

6. Knives are to meat as _____ are to paper.

7. Ants are to insects as _____ are to birds.

8. Strings are to violins as keys are to _____.

9. Potatoes are to stews as _____ are to salads.

10. Ice is to cubes as bread is to _____.

Word Clues Write the list word that fits each clue.

11. These animals roamed all over the West. _____

12. These are often black rectangles with white dots. _____

13. You might hear these in a huge canyon. _____

14. These people enforce the law. _____

15. These people may steal from you. _____

16. You don't want to be close when these erupt. _____

17. These are in charge of tribes or companies. _____

18. People have these about topics such as politics. _____

19. Organizations such as schools have these. _____

20. We use this word to describe us. _____

 Home Activity Your child learned to spell words that are irregular plurals. Locate three irregular plurals in a newspaper. Say the singular forms of the words and ask your child to spell the plurals.

Name _____

Vowel Sounds with *r*

Spelling Words				
snore	tornado	spare	appear	career
square	report	prepare	pioneer	chair
beware	smear	repair	sword	ignore
order	engineer	resort	volunteer	declare

Word Search Circle ten hidden list words. Words are down, across, and diagonal. Write the words on the lines.

```
F  V  W  P  P  R  R  E  S  O
S  W  O  R  D  E  E  N  N  R
M  L  A  L  E  S  P  G  P  E
E  Q  W  I  U  L  O  I  S  P
A  R  I  A  T  N  R  N  N  T
R  E  S  O  R  T  T  E  O  Y
A  T  E  P  O  R  D  E  R  B
W  O  H  S  Q  U  A  R  E  E
T  R  S  A  I  P  Z  E  N  R
Z  B  E  W  A  R  E  A  S  E
```

1. _____   6. _____

2. _____   7. _____

3. _____   8. _____

4. _____   9. _____

5. _____   10. _____

Synonyms Write the list word that has the same or nearly the same meaning.

11. twister _____   16. fix _____

12. ready _____   17. overlook _____

13. occupation _____   18. seem _____

14. announce _____   19. extra _____

15. seat _____   20. pathfinder _____

School + Home **Home Activity** Your child learned to spell words that have vowel sounds with *r*. Select three words from your child's spelling list and make up a sentence with him or her. Ask your child to write the sentence.

Name _____

Final Syllables *-en, -an, -el, -le, -il*

Spelling Words				
example	level	slogan	quarrel	scramble
evil	oxygen	wooden	double	travel
cancel	chuckle	fossil	toboggan	veteran
chisel	suburban	single	sudden	beagle

Words in Context Write the word to complete each sentence.

1. I _____ when I hear an amusing joke.

2. You must _____ your appointment if you can't make it.

3. Breathe deeply to get plenty of _____.

4. Sailing is a(n) _____ of a water sport.

5. Molly's _____ is a friendly, cheerful dog.

6. The boys went down the snowy hill on a(n) _____.

7. A sculptor uses a(n) _____ to shape marble.

8. The scientist found a(n) _____ of a dinosaur in the ground.

9. People can _____ in cars, trains, and planes.

10. Baseball players use a(n) _____ bat.

11. Shall we fry, poach, or _____ the eggs?

12. The company's _____ was easy to remember.

Antonyms Write the list word that has the opposite or nearly the opposite meaning.

13. newcomer   _____

14. agree   _____

15. rural   _____

16. married   _____

17. good   _____

18. uneven   _____

19. gradual   _____

20. single   _____

Home Activity Your child learned to spell words with the final syllables *-en, -an, -el, -le,* and *-il.* To practice at home, dictate a word with each final syllable. Ask your child to spell the word and provide a synonym or antonym for it.

29

Final Syllables -er, -ar, -or

Spelling Words				
danger	wander	tractor	dollar	harbor
eager	eraser	surrender	solar	sticker
locker	helicopter	pillar	refrigerator	caterpillar
rumor	glimmer	linger	sensor	alligator

Analogies Write the word that completes each comparison.

1. Hot is to oven as cold is to _____.

2. Page is to book as penny is to _____.

3. Flower is to bud as butterfly is to _____.

4. Moon is to lunar as sun is to _____.

5. Clothes are to closet as books are to _____.

6. Walk is to stroll as roam is to _____.

7. Patio is to yard as port is to _____.

8. Fingernail is to finger as _____ is to pencil.

9. Fact is to fiction as truth is to _____.

10. Sail is to ship as fly is to _____.

Hidden Words Each of these small words can be found inside one of the list words. Write the list word that contains the small word.

11. in   _____   16. end   _____

12. tick   _____   17. ill   _____

13. act   _____   18. so   _____

14. me   _____   19. an   _____

15. all   _____   20. age   _____

School + Home
Home Activity Your child learned to spell words with the final syllables -er, -ar, and -or. Choose a word with each final syllable from your child's spelling list. Ask your child to spell the word and use it in a sentence.

Name _____

Words with Schwa

Word Clues Write the list word that fits each clue.

1. This may have rides, contests, costumes, and parades.

2. This type of place has palm trees and year-round warm weather.

3. This is a type of board for special announcements.

4. This is what you do at birthdays, anniversaries, and holidays.

5. This is a time that is not yesterday or today.

6. This is where royalty lives and rules.

7. This green vegetable has long, crisp stalks.

8. This is anything with fancy, classic style.

9. This is what you do when you draw pictures.

10. This is a kind of nightwear.

1. _____
2. _____
3. _____
4. _____
5. _____
6. _____
7. _____
8. _____
9. _____
10. _____

Words in Context Write the list word that best completes each sentence.

11. The national _____ is a counting of everyone who lives in the U.S.

12. Can you _____ the number of students in your school?

13. Our car needs to be put in the _____ for the night.

14. We'll need to fill the tank with _____.

15. That _____ makes parts for lawnmowers.

16. Air conditioning is used in places with lots of heat and _____.

17. The doctor had to _____ on me to remove my appendix.

18. A diamond is a valuable and precious _____.

19. The largest city in Illinois is _____.

20. That was one _____ roller coaster ride!

11. _____
12. _____
13. _____
14. _____
15. _____
16. _____
17. _____
18. _____
19. _____
20. _____

Home Activity Your child wrote words with the schwa sound. Ask your child to spell three list words, telling you where the schwa sound is in each word.

Name _____

Words with Schwa

Proofread a Letter Laura wrote this letter to her aunt. Circle six spelling errors. Write the words correctly. Find one punctuation error. Write the sentence correctly.

Dear Aunt Betty,
    Next week we will celabrate at the carnaval. We've been decorating a float. Our theme will be the city of Chicago. The city has many eligant buildings. We want to illestrate this on our float. We were a little off on our estamate of how long it would take to complete it. It probly won't be easy, to get this beautiful, decorated platform out of the garage. Even so, we are looking forward to a terrific day!

1. _____   2. _____

3. _____   4. _____

5. _____   6. _____

7. _____

_____

Proofread Words Circle the correct spelling of the list word.

8. We moved to a _____ climate this winter.

tropecal   tropical   troppicle

9. The _____ made people feel sticky when they went outside.

humidity   humiduty   humidety

10. My favorite _____ have feet in them.

pajammas   pajamers   pajamas

11. The _____ shows that the population of our town has doubled.

sensus   census   censis

12. The weather _____ says that snow is on the way!

bullatin   bulliten   bulletin

Home Activity Your child identified misspelled words with schwa. Have your child tell you the three hardest words and then spell the words aloud.

32

Name _____

Compound Words

Complete the Sentence Write the list word that best completes the sentence.

1. Do you know that three teaspoons equal one ____?

2. The ____ is a place where justice is tested every day.

3. The ant stored food while the ____ played.

4. When you're away for a while, it is common to feel ____.

5. The hum from a ____ comes from its rapidly beating wings.

6. Some people wear a ____ to sleep on an airplane.

7. The ____ is full of exotic plants.

8. The circle of light on the stage was from the ____.

9. I like to walk ____ in the wet sand.

10. The ____ was full of old news clippings and photos.

1. _____

2. _____

3. _____

4. _____

5. _____

6. _____

7. _____

8. _____

9. _____

10. _____

Definitions Answer each clue with a list word. Write it on the line.

11. hills, trees, and lakes

12. not heavy at all

13. carries a message

14. hang something with it

15. stays dry

16. shaking ground

17. boat with oars

18. worm holder

19. one-third of a tablespoon

20. circling water

11. _____

12. _____

13. _____

14. _____

15. _____

16. _____

17. _____

18. _____

19. _____

20. _____

Home Activity Your child used the meanings of list words to write them in sentences and match them with synonyms. Ask your child to tell you what a compound word is and give three examples.

Compound Words

Proofread a Letter Halie wrote a letter home from camp. There are seven spelling errors and one capitalization error. Circle the errors and write the corrections on the lines.

Dear Mom and Dad,

    I'm not crying or homsick. This paper got a little wet because I'm in a rowboat. I have a fish hook on the line. The countryside around camp is awesome. We run around bearfoot most days. My Counselor is the nature teacher. Yesterday, everybody saw a hummbird. The camp has a greenhouse where all the vegetables we eat are grown. Thanks for the waterproff slicker. It's litewait and will keep me dry. You sent a really beautiful postcard of the Grand Canyon. I used a thumtack to hang it on my bunk wall!

                Write soon,
                Halie

Spelling Words

waterproof
teaspoon
grasshopper
homesick
barefoot
courthouse
earthquake
rowboat
scrapbook
countryside

lightweight
fishhook
spotlight
blindfold
whirlpool
tablespoon
greenhouse
postcard
hummingbird
thumbtack

1. _____
2. _____
3. _____
4. _____
5. _____
6. _____
7. _____
8. _____

Proofread Words Correct the spellings of the list words. Write the words correctly on the lines.

9. Meet me on the steps of the <u>corthouse</u>.   9. _____

10. My <u>scapebook</u> is full of pictures and mementos.   10. _____

11. Performers love to be in the <u>spotelite</u>.   11. _____

12. The bathwater went down the drain in a little <u>wirlpool</u>.   12. _____

13. Pictures fell off the wall during the <u>erthkwake</u>.   13. _____

14. I folded my scarf into a <u>blindefold</u>.   14. _____

15. A <u>grasshoper</u> has long, strong legs.   15. _____

Frequently Misspelled Words

something
everybody
everyone

Home Activity Your child identified misspelled compound words. Ask your child to spell three of the compound words for you.

34

Name _____

Name _____

Consonant Sounds /j/, /ks/, /sk/, and /s/

Spelling Words				
excuse	scene	muscle	explore	pledge
journal	science	schedule	gigantic	scheme
Japan	excellent	exclaim	fascinate	ginger
scholar	scent	dodge	smudge	schooner

Classify Write the list word that best completes the group.

1. plan, plot, _____

2. avoid, elude, sidestep, _____

3. diary, log, magazine, _____

4. setting, landscape, _____

5. aroma, perfume, odor, _____

6. captivate, interest, _____

7. bone, skin, _____

8. yacht, kayak, _____

9. outstanding, brilliant, _____

10. basil, oregano, _____

1. _____

2. _____

3. _____

4. _____

5. _____

6. _____

7. _____

8. _____

9. _____

10. _____

Words in Context Write the list word that completes each sentence.

11. Tokyo is the largest city in _____.

12. Cry out and _____ mean the same thing.

13. A _____ enjoys learning and studying.

14. The bad weather is my _____ for being late today.

15. Astronauts _____ outer space.

16. I'll add the meeting to my _____.

17. I made a donation _____ to the local charity.

18. My _____ book contains many experiments.

19. The _____ on the wall is from finger paint.

20. The redwood trees in California are _____.

11. _____

12. _____

13. _____

14. _____

15. _____

16. _____

17. _____

18. _____

19. _____

20. _____

 Home Activity Your child wrote words with special spellings for certain consonant sounds. Have your child pick the five most difficult words for him or her. Go over the spellings of these words with your child.

Name _____

Consonant Sounds /j/, /ks/, /sk/, and /s/

Proofread a Travel Poster There are seven spelling errors and one punctuation error. Circle the errors and write the corrections on the lines.

Spelling Words

excuse
scene
muscle
explore
pledge
journal
science
schedule
gigantic
scheme

Japan
excellent
exclaim
fascinate
ginger
scholar
scent
dodge
smudge
schooner

1. _____   2. _____

3. _____   4. _____

5. _____   6. _____

7. _____

8. _____

Proofread Words Circle the correct spelling of the list word.

9. plege   pleje   pledge

10. sceme   scheme   skeme

11. smudge   smuge   smuje

12. mussle   muscel   muscle

13. dodje   dodge   dogde

14. journal   journle   jurnal

15. jigantic   gidgantic   gigantic

16. skooner   schooner   scooner

Frequently Misspelled Words

except
excited
school

 School + Home **Home Activity** Your child identified misspelled list words. Review the *sch* and *sc* words and their pronunciations with your child.

Name_____

One Consonant or Two

Words in Context Write the list word that best completes the sentence.

1. The vegetable ____ looks like little trees.   1. _____

2. It was hard to cross the street because of the police ____.   2. _____

3. The capital of ____ is Nashville.   3. _____

4. Don't forget to button your ____.   4. _____

5. "Faster, faster," he urged the horse as it began to ____.   5. _____

6. He looked in the ____ to comb his hair.   6. _____

7. The ____ River is the second-longest river in the United States.   7. _____

8. Our class has ____ after lunch.   8. _____

9. Do you get a weekly ____ for doing chores?   9. _____

10. I need your telephone number and ____ for our records.   10. _____

Antonyms Write the list word that has the opposite or nearly the opposite meaning.

11. scatter   11. _____

12. delayed   12. _____

13. obey   13. _____

14. disregard   14. _____

15. remove   15. _____

Synonyms Write the list word that has the same or almost the same meaning.

16. declare   16. _____

17. group   17. _____

18. foe   18. _____

19. summer squash   19. _____

20. succeed   20. _____

Home Activity Your child wrote words with double consonants. Take turns saying and spelling the list words aloud.

Name _____

One Consonant or Two

Proofread a Newspaper Article Circle six misspelled words. Write the words correctly. Find one capitalization error. Write the sentence correctly.

> Something odd hapenned in the students' dining room. Some students wanted brocoli at every meal. Their oponents wanted zuchinni. A commitee was formed. They decided to take a vote. No one expected an immediat result. The committee had something surprising to announce. most of the students preferred carrots!

1. _____   2. _____

3. _____   4. _____

5. _____   6. _____

7. _____

Proofread Words Circle the correct spelling of the list words.

8. Memphis and Nashville are cities in ____.

Tenessee   Tennese   Tennessee

9. Most students love ____ after being inside.

recess   reccess   recces

10. I ____ a collection of old comic books.

posess   possess   posses

11. The settlers used a wooden plank to ____ the door.

barricade   barricad   bariccade

12. I am hoping to ____ a lot this school year.

acomplish   accomplish   accommplish

13. The bathroom ____ was foggy because of the steam from the shower.

mirrer   miror   mirror

14. I will ____ the winner at the end of the game.

announce   anounce   anounnce

Spelling Words

address
collar
mirror
recess
committee
collect
Mississippi
immediate
command
appreciate

announce
possess
Tennessee
gallop
opponent
barricade
broccoli
accomplish
allowance
zucchini

Frequently Misspelled Words

different
happened

Home Activity Your child identified misspelled list words. Have your child tell you the three most difficult list words and then spell them to you.

Name _____

Prefixes *un-*, *de-*, *dis-*

Spelling Words				
uncover	defrost	uncomfortable	discourage	disadvantage
unfortunate	unfamiliar	disability	discomfort	deodorant
unemployed	deflate	disbelief	unpredictable	disapprove
disappoint	unpleasant	dehydrated	disqualify	undecided

Definitions in Context Write the list word that has the same or almost the same meaning as the underlined word or words.

1. Moisture is removed from <u>dried out</u> food.   1. _____

2. I need to <u>melt</u> the turkey.   2. _____

3. It was <u>unlucky</u> that I broke my leg.   3. _____

4. My mother has been <u>out of work</u> since the factory closed. 4. _____

5. The outcome of the contest was <u>in doubt</u> for months.   5. _____

6. The player's tardiness was a <u>difficulty</u> for the team.   6. _____

7. I took a route home from school that was <u>new</u> to me.   7. _____

8. The roller coaster ride was <u>disagreeable</u> to me.   8. _____

9. It was <u>painful</u> to sleep on the old, lumpy mattress.   9. _____

10. The team decided to <u>ban</u> a player for cheating.   10. _____

Antonyms Write the list word that has the opposite or nearly the opposite meaning.

11. ability   11. _____

12. with odor   12. _____

13. belief   13. _____

14. expected   14. _____

15. please   15. _____

16. inflate   16. _____

17. conceal   17. _____

18. support   18. _____

19. encourage   19. _____

20. comfortable   20. _____

School + Home **Home Activity** Your child wrote words with prefixes. Say a prefix and have your child respond with one word from the list that has that prefix.

Name _____

Prefixes *un-*, *de-*, *dis-*

Proofread an Article There are seven spelling errors and one capitalization error. Circle the errors and write the corrections on the lines.

Spelling Words

uncover
defrost
uncomfortable
discourage
disadvantage
unfortunate
unfamiliar
disability
discomfort
deodorant

unemployed
deflate
disbelief
unpredictable
disapprove
disappoint
unpleasant
dehydrated
disqualify
undecided

A Very Long Race

Many look upon marathon runners with disbeleaf. These athletes run 26 miles in unfamilar cities. They deal with unpredictible and sometimes unplesant weather. Many run with discomfort and some with a disbility. Many runners become dehidrated. Spectators do not disapoint the runners. They give cups of water to all Runners.

1. _____   2. _____

3. _____   4. _____

5. _____   6. _____

7. _____

8. _____

Proofread Words Circle the correct spelling of the list word.

9. deordorent   deodorant   deoderant

10. disqualify   disqualyfie   dequalify

11. uncomfortible   unconfortable   uncomfortable

12. deflate   deflait   defleat

13. deapprove   disapprove   disaprove

14. disadvantadge   disadvantige   disadvantage

15. undecided   indecided   undecide

16. discomfrt   discomfort   discomefrt

Frequently Misspelled Words

until
before

School + Home

Home Activity Your child identified misspelled list words. Ask your child to name one word for each prefix studied and spell the word.

40

Words with Schwa

Spelling Words				
jewel	kingdom	gasoline	factory	garage
tropical	pajamas	estimate	tomorrow	humidity
Chicago	bulletin	carnival	illustrate	elegant
census	terrific	celebrate	operate	celery

Synonyms Write the list word that has the same or nearly the same meaning.

1. great _____

2. festival _____

3. count _____

4. carport _____

5. tasteful _____

6. gem _____

7. rejoice _____

8. nightclothes _____

9. moisture _____

10. guess _____

Scramble Unscramble the list words and write them on the lines.

11. seloaing _____

12. slurtileat _____

13. tublelin _____

14. wormorto _____

15. plorcita _____

16. troycaf _____

17. torapee _____

18. coaCgih _____

19. midkong _____

20. rylcee _____

School + Home **Home Activity** Your child learned to spell words with the schwa sound. Ask your child to name three words with this sound and spell them.

Compound Words

Spelling Words				
waterproof	teaspoon	grasshopper	homesick	barefoot
courthouse	earthquake	rowboat	scrapbook	countryside
lightweight	fishhook	spotlight	blindfold	whirlpool
tablespoon	greenhouse	postcard	hummingbird	thumbtack

Analogies Write the word that completes each comparison.

1. Urban is to city as rural is to _____.

2. Short is to tall as heavy is to _____.

3. Librarian is to library as judge is to _____.

4. Animal is to zoo as plant is to _____.

5. Snake is to reptile as _____ is to insect.

6. Glue is to tape as nail is to _____.

7. Pedal is to bicycle as oar is to _____.

8. Scarf is to neck as _____ is to eyes.

9. Cup is to china as _____ is to silverware.

10. E-mail is to computer as _____ is to mailbox.

Word Clues Write the list word that fits each clue.

11. This might describe a raincoat and boots. _____

12. Cooks use this to measure ingredients. _____

13. Make this to remember a special trip. _____

14. Don't become an actor if you don't like this. _____

15. You can feed this in your backyard. _____

16. A big one might cause buildings to fall. _____

17. Beware of this when swimming in a big lake or river. _____

18. Going away to summer camp might make you feel like this. _____

19. Walk this way at the beach if you like sand between your toes. _____

20. Put this on the end of your line. _____

Home Activity Your child learned to spell compound words. Find four compound words in a magazine. Write all the words in the compounds in random order. Ask your child to put the correct words together to make the compound words.

Consonant Sounds /j/, /ks/, /sk/, and /s/

Spelling Words				
excuse	scene	muscle	explore	pledge
journal	science	schedule	gigantic	scheme
Japan	excellent	exclaim	fascinate	ginger
scholar	scent	dodge	smudge	schooner

Word Search Circle ten hidden list words. Words are down, across, and diagonal. Write the words on the lines.

```
F  V  S  C  H  E  D  U  L  E
E  X  C  L  A  I  M  N  N  R
C  D  H  M  G  I  N  G  E  R
K  Q  O  I  U  L  O  I  S  S
E  R  L  D  T  S  S  N  M  C
D  E  A  O  G  T  C  E  U  I
U  X  R  P  O  E  E  L  R  E
L  C  H  E  O  U  N  R  E  N
S  C  H  O  O  N  E  R  N  C
Z  F  A  S  C  I  N  A  T  E
```

1. _____   6. _____

2. _____   7. _____

3. _____   8. _____

4. _____   9. _____

5. _____   10. _____

Hidden Words Each of these small words can be found inside one of the list words. Write the list word that contains the small word.

11. ant _____   16. our _____

12. cell _____   17. aim _____

13. mud _____   18. edge _____

14. use _____   19. hem _____

15. pan _____   20. cent _____

Home Activity Your child learned to spell words with various consonant sounds. Ask your child to write two words in which the *sk* sound is spelled in different ways.

One Consonant or Two

Spelling Words				
address	collar	mirror	recess	committee
collect	Mississippi	immediate	command	appreciate
announce	possess	Tennessee	gallop	opponent
barricade	broccoli	accomplish	allowance	zucchini

Analogies Write the word that completes each comparison.

1. Jog is to run as trot is to _____.

2. Pecan is to nut as _____ is to squash.

3. Speak is to talk as own is to _____.

4. Friend is to enemy as teammate is to _____.

5. Car is to tire as shirt is to _____.

6. President is to company as chairman is to _____.

7. Open is to close as discard is to _____.

8. Car is to automobile as obstacle is to _____.

9. Cut is to scissors as reflect is to _____.

10. Yell is to shout as proclaim is to _____.

Word Clues Write the list word that fits each clue.

11. a break in the school day   _____

12. the second-longest river in the United States   _____

13. to make an effort and succeed   _____

14. your street number and name and city   _____

15. a green vegetable with stalks and florets   _____

16. a general's job in the army   _____

17. money received each week   _____

18. a state that borders Kentucky   _____

19. to value and treasure   _____

20. happening right now   _____

 Home Activity Your child learned to spell words with double consonants. To practice at home, dictate three words with double consonants. Have your child write them.

Prefixes *un-, de-, dis-*

Spelling Words

uncover	defrost	uncomfortable	discourage	disadvantage
unfortunate	unfamiliar	disability	discomfort	deodorant
unemployed	deflate	disbelief	unpredictable	disapprove
disappoint	unpleasant	dehydrated	disqualify	undecided

Synonyms Write the list word that has the same or nearly the same meaning.

1. jobless _____
2. strange _____
3. handicap _____
4. reject _____
5. uneasiness _____

6. expose _____
7. doubt _____
8. bar _____
9. dried _____
10. changeable _____

Analogies Write the word that completes each comparison.

11. Fix is to break as freeze is to _____.

12. Easy is to difficult as lucky is to _____.

13. Happy is to sad as relaxed is to _____.

14. Soap is to cleanser as antiperspirant is to _____.

15. Mad is to angry as uncertain is to _____.

16. Drain is to pool as _____ is to balloon.

17. Freedom is to liberty as weakness is to _____.

18. Beautiful is to ugly as charming is to _____.

19. Help is to support as frustrate is to _____.

20. Please is to annoy as encourage is to _____.

School + Home

Home Activity Your child learned to spell words with the prefixes *un-*, *de-*, and *dis-*. Find three words with these prefixes in a newspaper. Ask your child to spell each word and name a word that means the opposite.

Words from Many Cultures

Spelling Words				
khaki	hula	banana	ballet	waltz
tomato	vanilla	canyon	yogurt	banquet
macaroni	polka	cobra	koala	barbecue
safari	buffet	stampede	karate	kiosk

Word Histories Write a list word for each description.

1. This is French for a table full of different foods.

1. _____

2. Many students practice this Japanese form of self-defense.

2. _____

3. Native Americans introduced this fruit to the settlers.

3. _____

4. This is a Turkish treat made from milk.

4. _____

5. This Polynesian dance is usually performed in a grass skirt.

5. _____

6. This is a Spanish word for a large group of running buffaloes or horses.

6. _____

7. Although it has a French name, this dance form started in Russia.

7. _____

8. This furry animal has kept its Australian name.

8. _____

9. Soldiers wear this yellowish brown fabric named by the Persians and Hindus so they can't be easily seen.

9. _____

10. This partner dance means "to turn" in German.

10. _____

11. This is an Italian name for a well-known pasta.

11. _____

12. The Spanish and Portuguese used the same name for this yellow fruit.

12. _____

13. A Native American word is used to name this kind of outside cooking.

13. _____

14. This Polish dance is very lively.

14. _____

15. Although this word is Arabic, this type of journey is done in Africa.

15. _____

16. The Spanish named this flavorful type of bean long before there was ice cream.

16. _____

17. This word for a feast or a formal dinner comes from French.

17. _____

18. This is a Spanish word for a very deep valley carved out by a river.

18. _____

19. The name for this hooded, poisonous snake comes from the Portuguese.

19. _____

20. This is a Turkish word for a newsstand.

20. _____

School + Home

Home Activity Your child wrote words from other cultures. Go over the pronunciation of the French words *buffet* and *ballet*. Remind your child that in French *-et* in these words is pronounced as long *a*.

Words from Many Cultures

Proofread a Poster Circle the seven spelling errors in the school poster.
Write the words correctly. Write the last sentence, using correct punctuation.

Our New After-School Programs

Learn to Dance
- poka and Texas two-step
- ballet (with tutus and toe shoes)
- walts and other ballroom dances
- hula and dances of the Pacific

Learn Martial Arts
- karatie • judo • kung fu

Learn How to Cook
- barbecue sauces
- tomatoe salads
- homemade yogurt
- macaronie and cheese and other pastas
- bananana cream pie and other desserts

Sign up at the kyosk outside the office.
Bring a permission form from your parents?

Spelling Words
khaki
hula
banana
ballet
waltz
tomato
vanilla
canyon
yogurt
banquet
macaroni
polka
cobra
koala
barbecue
safari
buffet
stampede
karate
kiosk

1. _____   2. _____

3. _____   4. _____

5. _____   6. _____

7. _____

8. _____

Frequently Misspelled Words
our
again

Proofread Words Circle the correct spelling of the list word.
Write the word.

9. The frightened cattle started to ____.   9. _____

    stamped   stampede   stampeed

10. I love the assortment of foods on the restaurant ____.   10. _____

    buffet   buffay   buffee

School + Home   **Home Activity** Your child identified misspelled list words. Say a list word and spell it incorrectly. Ask your child to spell the word correctly.

Name _____

Prefixes *over-*, *under-*, *sub-*, *super-*, *out-*

Spelling Words				
overlook	underline	subway	subset	supermarket
outlet	underground	overboard	undercurrent	superstar
overtime	supersonic	submarine	undercover	overcast
outfield	output	supernatural	subdivision	subhead

Classifying Write the list word that belongs in each group.

1. city, trains, underground, ____

2. sky, clouds, gray, ____

3. diamond, mound, infield, ____

4. police officer, disguise, ____

5. grocery, bakery, butcher, ____

6. daydream, forget, omit, ____

7. highlight, line, ____

8. plane, jet engine, speed of sound, ____

9. work, extra hours, ____

10. performer, actor, singer, ____

1. _____

2. _____

3. _____

4. _____

5. _____

6. _____

7. _____

8. _____

9. _____

10. _____

Definitions Write the list word that fits each definition.

11. This is part of a community.

12. This is the result of production.

13. This means eerie and ghostly.

14. This is a small part of a larger group.

15. This means beneath the earth.

16. This is a vessel that travels underwater.

17. This comes under a heading.

18. This is a pull under the waves.

19. This means falling off a ship.

20. This can be a store that offers discounts.

11. _____

12. _____

13. _____

14. _____

15. _____

16. _____

17. _____

18. _____

19. _____

20. _____

Home Activity Your child wrote words with prefixes. Ask your child to name four words and tell you how the prefixes in each word affect its meaning.

Name _____

Prefixes over-, under-, sub-, super-, out-

Proofread a Paragraph Circle six spelling errors. Write the words correctly.
Find one punctuation error and write the sentence using the correct
punctuation.

> If you had a choice, would you want to break the sound
> barrier in a super sonic jet? Is cruising beneath the
> surface of the sea in a sub marine more your style?
> What about riding underground on a large sub way
> system? Would you rather stay all night in a deserted
> house waiting for something super natural to happen? Do
> you like sports. Perhaps you'd really rather be playing
> ball in the out field? Fortunately, one doesn't have to be
> a super star to do any of these things.

1. _____	2. _____
3. _____	4. _____
5. _____	6. _____
7. _____	

Proofread Words Circle the word that is spelled correctly.

8.	submarine	submareen	submarein
9.	subdivsion	subdivison	subdivision
10.	subersonic	supersonic	supresonic
11.	underline	undeline	undrline
12.	outfeild	outfeeld	outfield
13.	overcast	overcas	ovrcast
14.	overlok	overlook	ovarlock
15.	suparmarkit	suprmarkat	supermarket
16.	overboard	overbored	ovarboard

Spelling Words

overlook
underline
subway
subset
supermarket
outlet
underground
overboard
undercurrent
superstar

overtime
supersonic
submarine
undercover
overcast
outfield
output
supernatural
subdivision
subhead

**Frequently
Misspelled
Words**

outside
because

Home Activity Your child identified misspelled list words. Ask your child to tell you which three words
are most difficult and then have your child spell them with you.

49

Name _____

Homophones

Spelling Words				
cent	sent	scent	threw	through
weather	whether	their	there	they're
chili	chilly	tide	tied	pale
pail	aloud	allowed	course	coarse

Words in Context Write homophones to complete the sentences.

On a **(1)**____ day, hot, spicy **(2)**____ with cheese really tastes good.

1. _____   2. _____

We made sure the boats were **(3)**____ down securely against the rising **(4)**____.

3. _____   4. _____

The **(5)**____ will determine **(6)**____ or not we play the game.

5. _____   6. _____

I **(7)**____ away for that special one- **(8)**____ offer for my favorite perfume **(9)**____.

7. _____   8. _____   9. _____

Speaking **(10)**____ is not **(11)**____ in the library.

10. _____   11. _____

You **(12)**____ the ball so far that it went **(13)**____ the window!

12. _____   13. _____

(14)____ starting **(15)**____ lemonade business over **(16)**____ near the bakery.

14. _____   15. _____   16. _____

The golf **(17)**____ is designed to be challenging. It has sand, water traps, woods, and smooth and **(18)**____ grass.

17. _____   18. _____

The **(19)**____ child carried the **(20)**____ onto the beach.

19. _____   20. _____

Home Activity Your child learned to use homophones in context. Ask your child to make up other sentences using list words.

Homophones

Proofread an Ad Circle six spelling errors. Write the words correctly.
Find one capitalization error. Write the sentence correctly.

> On a chilly day, shout allowed for our delicious chilly!
> It will warm you through and threw! Ask about our
> ninety-nine sent special. If the whether is bad, call us. We
> Deliver for free! Of course, their is no finer tasting treat!

1. _____   2. _____

3. _____   4. _____

5. _____   6. _____

7. _____

Proofread Words Circle the correct spelling of the list word. Write the word.

8. Burlap is a ____ fabric.

   corse   cuarse   coarse   8. _____

9. I think ____ going on a class trip tomorrow.

   they're   their   they'ar   9. _____

10. Sky blue is a ____ color.

    pail   pale   paile   10. _____

11. Your perfume has a lovely ____.

    scent   cent   sent   11. _____

12. I am not sure ____ I can go.

    wheather   whether   weather   12. _____

13. The sailor ____ down the ship's hatch.

    tide   teid   tied   13. _____

14. The candy cost one ____.

    scent   cent   sent   14. _____

15. The score was even and the game was ____.

    tide   teid   tied   15. _____

Home Activity Your child identified misspelled and misused homophones. Say a homophone in a sentence and have your child spell it.

Spelling Words

cent
sent
scent
threw
through
weather
whether
their
there
they're

chili
chilly
tide
tied
pale
pail
aloud
allowed
course
coarse

Frequently Misspelled Words

their
there
they're

Name _____

Suffixes *-ible*, *-able*

Synonyms Write the list word that has the same or nearly the same meaning.

1. in style   1. _____

2. bendable   2. _____

3. welcoming   3. _____

4. ridiculous   4. _____

5. car with top down   5. _____

6. positive   6. _____

7. permissible   7. _____

8. able to turn inside out   8. _____

9. can be cleaned   9. _____

10. accountable   10. _____

Antonyms Write the list word that has the opposite or nearly the opposite meaning.

11. memorable   11. _____

12. unfriendly   12. _____

13. disagreeable   13. _____

14. unreasonable   14. _____

15. unbreakable   15. _____

16. unavailable   16. _____

17. intolerable   17. _____

18. can't be divided   18. _____

19. foolish   19. _____

20. worthless   20. _____

Home Activity Your child used meanings to select list words that were synonyms and antonyms. Have your child tell you the meaning of three list words and spell the words.

52

Name _____

Suffixes *-ible, -able*

Proofread an Article Find five spelling errors and one capitalization error in the article. Circle the errors and write the corrections on the lines.

> ### Fashion Sense
>
> Store buyers are responsible for ordering fashionible clothing customers will like. Last year, mrs. Clark, the store buyer, ordered dozens of reversible sweaters. The sweaters were washible, availible in a variety of colors, and sold at a reasonible price. When the sweaters sold out quickly, the buyer knew she had made a sensable choice.

1. _____   2. _____

3. _____   4. _____

5. _____   6. _____

Proofread Words Circle the correct spelling of the list word.

7. The gymnast is as ____ as a rubber band.

   flexable   flexibel   flexible

8. Porcelain china is delicate and ____.

   breakable   brakeable   breakible

9. Be ____ to your guests when they visit.

   hospital   hospitable   hospitible

10. I'd love to have a car with a ____ top.

    convertible   convertable   convertibel

11. Sixty-three is ____ by seven.

    dividable   divisable   divisible

12. Eat three ____ and balanced meals every day.

    sensible   sensable   senseable

Home Activity Your child identified misspelled list words. Ask your child to spell three list words that end in *-ible* and three list words that end in *-able*.

Spelling Words

sensible
washable
available
agreeable
fashionable
valuable
flexible
reasonable
favorable
breakable

convertible
forgettable
laughable
sociable
allowable
divisible
hospitable
reversible
responsible
tolerable

Frequently Misspelled Words

when
then
went

Name _____

Negative Prefixes

Spelling Words				
invisible	illiterate	irregular	irresistible	impossible
informal	illegal	impatient	independent	incorrect
inactive	imperfect	impolite	immature	illogical
indefinite	inappropriate	immobile	irresponsible	inexpensive

Missing Words Write the missing list word.

1. If you learn to read, you are not ____.

2. If you have good manners, you'll rarely be ____.

3. If you earn a living, you can be ____.

4. If you have a "can do" attitude, little is ____.

5. If you're always trustworthy, you are never ____.

6. If you always follow the law, then you never do anything ____.

7. If you're always right, then you're never ____.

8. If you always act responsibly, then you are not ____.

9. If you set an exact time to meet, it is not ____.

10. If something always makes sense, it is not ____.

1. _____

2. _____

3. _____

4. _____

5. _____

6. _____

7. _____

8. _____

9. _____

10. _____

Classifying Write the list word that completes the group.

11. cheap, reasonable, low-cost, ____

12. flawed, faulty, defective, ____

13. restless, fidgety, ____

14. unseen, faint, ____

15. casual, relaxed, ____

16. idle, quiet, immobile, ____

17. out of place, unsuitable, ____

18. stationary, motionless, ____

19. tempting, appealing, enticing, ____

20. uneven, lopsided, ____

11. _____

12. _____

13. _____

14. _____

15. _____

16. _____

17. _____

18. _____

19. _____

20. _____

Home Activity Your child wrote words with prefixes. Ask your child to spell one word for each of the four negative prefixes.

Negative Prefixes

Proofread a Speech Circle six spelling errors in the toymaker's speech.
Write the words correctly. Write the run-on sentence as two sentences.

"I want to create an irresistable toy for children. It will make the user innvisible. I need five independent teams to work on this. As always, I am impashent to get this project started! We do not have an indefinute amount of time. I'm hoping to have this toy on the market by the end of the year. Does anyone have any questions? Does anyone think this task is ilogical or inpossible to do? Do we all agree this can be done let's get to work!"

1. _____   2. _____

3. _____   4. _____

5. _____   6. _____

7. _____

_____

Spelling Words

invisible
illiterate
irregular
irresistible
impossible
informal
illegal
impatient
independent
incorrect

inactive
imperfect
impolite
immature
illogical
indefinite
inappropriate
immobile
irresponsible
inexpensive

Proofread Words Circle the word that is spelled correctly.

8. irresistible   unresistable   ilresistable

9. ilexpensive   imexpensive   inexpensive

10. inmature   immature   imature

11. imperfect   ilperfect   unperfect

12. imdependent   independent   ildependent

13. imactive   innactive   inactive

14. impolite   inpolite   unpolite

15. illiterate   iliterate   inliterate

16. imappropriate   inappropriate   inapropriate

Frequently Misspelled Words

through
always

Home Activity Your child identified misspelled list words. Take turns spelling list words that begin with the four negative prefixes studied.

55

Words from Many Cultures

Spelling Words				
khaki	waltz	yogurt	cobra	buffet
hula	tomato	banquet	koala	stampede
banana	vanilla	macaroni	barbecue	karate
ballet	canyon	polka	safari	kiosk

Alphabetize Write the ten list words below in alphabetical order.

kiosk	stampede
safari	buffet
koala	polka
banquet	karate
ballet	khaki

1. _____

2. _____

3. _____

4. _____

5. _____

6. _____

7. _____

8. _____

9. _____

10. _____

Classifying Write the list word that belongs in each group.

11. lettuce, carrots, onion, _____

12. dance, ballroom, elegant, _____

13. rattlesnake, boa constrictor, _____

14. spaghetti, noodles, pasta, _____

15. gorge, valley, ravine, _____

16. Hawaii, dance, grass skirt, _____

17. milk, creamy, fruit, _____

18. fruit, yellow, plant, _____

19. chocolate, strawberry, _____

20. food, outdoors, grill, _____

School + Home **Home Activity** Your child has learned to spell words that come from a variety of cultures. With your child, look up several of the words in a dictionary and discuss what the dictionary says about the words' origins.

Name _____

Prefixes *over-*, *under-*, *sub-*, *super-*, *out-*

Spelling Words				
overlook	supermarket	undercurrent	submarine	output
underline	outlet	superstar	undercover	supernatural
subway	underground	overtime	overcast	subdivision
subset	overboard	supersonic	outfield	subhead

Analogies Write the list word that completes each comparison.

1. Light is to heavy as sunny is to _____.

2. Title is to subtitle as head is to _____.

3. Sky is to airplane as ocean is to _____.

4. Carpenter is to house as baseball player is to _____.

5. Shoes are to shoe store as food is to _____.

6. Living room is to outside as cabin is to _____.

7. Street is to bus as underground is to _____.

8. Strong is to athlete as famous is to _____.

9. Comedian is to funny as ghost is to _____.

10. Store is to mall as house is to _____.

Synonyms Write the list word that has the same, or nearly the same, meaning.

11. underscore _____

12. secret _____

13. category _____

14. extra _____

15. production _____

16. hint _____

17. buried _____

18. socket _____

19. fast _____

20. forget _____

Home Activity Your child has completed analogies containing words with prefixes. Ask your child to make up two analogies containing words from the list and explain how the analogies work.

57

Name _____

Homophones

Crossword Puzzle Use the clues to find the list words. Write each letter in a box.

Across
2. gave permission
6. not here
7. fastened
8. pitched
9. place to play golf

Down
1. said so it could be heard
3. if
4. finished
5. smell
7. belonging to them

Classifying Write the list word that belongs in each group.

10. rain, snow, tornado, _____

11. cold, icy, frosty, _____

12. rough, thick, _____

13. taco, spaghetti, soup, _____

14. bucket, container, jug, _____

15. nickel, dime, quarter, _____

16. you're, we're, _____

17. white, colorless, sickly, _____

18. ocean, waves, high, low, _____

19. letter, mailed, transmitted, _____

Home Activity Your child has learned to spell homophones. Ask your child to find some of the list words in a newspaper or magazine. Then ask your child to spell one or more homophones for each word and use them in sentences.

Suffixes *-ible*, *-able*

Spelling Words				
sensible	fashionable	favorable	laughable	hospitable
washable	valuable	breakable	sociable	reversible
available	flexible	convertible	allowable	responsible
agreeable	reasonable	forgettable	divisible	tolerable

Words in Context Complete each sentence with a list word.

1. Be careful with that vase because it is _____.

2. It is hot in the desert, but the dry air makes it _____.

3. Jim's mom was _____ and invited us to stay for dinner.

4. You can wear the jacket with that side in or out because it is _____.

5. A(n) _____ car is not practical in a cold climate.

6. Anita didn't go to the party because she was not feeling _____.

7. Gold and silver are _____ metals.

8. The critic liked the movie, so he gave it a(n) _____ review.

9. Is that number _____ by ten?

10. It's all right to get your uniform muddy because it is _____.

11. The magician's tricks were so obvious they were _____.

12. The soccer team took care to make plays that were _____.

13. Lizzy often wears new styles because she likes to be _____.

14. I can't recall the story's characters because they were _____.

15. The Henrys asked Carla to baby-sit, but she was not _____ that day.

16. Unlike the unpleasant dog next door, our pet is always _____.

17. Who is _____ for setting the table?

18. It is _____ to wear sturdy shoes on a long hike.

19. If you work on the problem, you will think of a(n) _____ answer.

20. Rubber is used for many items because it is _____.

Home Activity Your child has learned to spell words with the suffixes *-ible* and *-able*. Ask your child to make up several sentences containing list words and to spell each list word used.

Negative Prefixes

Spelling Words				
invisible	impossible	independent	impolite	inappropriate
illiterate	informal	incorrect	immature	immobile
irregular	illegal	inactive	illogical	irresponsible
irresistible	impatient	imperfect	indefinite	inexpensive

Synonyms Write the list word that has the same, or nearly the same, meaning.

1. restless   _____

2. cheap   _____

3. rude   _____

4. motionless   _____

5. casual   _____

6. vague   _____

7. uneven   _____

8. lazy   _____

9. separate   _____

10. fascinating   _____

Antonyms Write the list word that has the opposite, or nearly the opposite, meaning.

11. lawful   _____

12. experienced   _____

13. excellent   _____

14. reasonable   _____

15. accurate   _____

16. educated   _____

17. suitable   _____

18. likely   _____

19. noticeable   _____

20. dependable   _____

Home Activity Your child has written synonyms and antonyms for words with negative prefixes. Name several list words. Ask your child to spell each word and to name a synonym and/or antonym for each.

Name _____

Multisyllabic Words

Spelling Words				
elementary	vehicle	miniature	probability	opportunity
substitute	variety	literature	elevator	Pennsylvania
ravioli	cafeteria	mosaic	tuxedo	meteorite
fascination	cylinder	intermediate	centennial	curiosity

Words in Context Write the list word that best completes each sentence.

1. I'm having lunch in the _____ today.

2. Did you know that cheese _____ is on the menu?

3. Eating a _____ of foods keeps you heathy.

4. Next year our town is 100 years old, so we'll have a _____ celebration.

5. The astronauts drove a lunar _____ on the moon.

6. The colorful _____ on the table top is made of tiny tiles.

7. A shooting star is really a falling _____.

8. The capital of _____ is Harrisburg.

9. The levels of swimming at my camp are beginner, _____, and advanced.

10. Books, poetry, and short stories are types of _____.

11. Let's take the _____ to the tenth floor.

12. We had a _____ teacher for one week.

13. He had a _____ with all types of model trains.

1. _____

2. _____

3. _____

4. _____

5. _____

6. _____

7. _____

8. _____

9. _____

10. _____

11. _____

12. _____

13. _____

Synonyms Write the list word that has the same or almost the same meaning as the word or phrase.

14. tube

15. tiny

16. basic

17. lucky chance

18. desire to know

19. formal suit

20. likelihood

14. _____

15. _____

16. _____

17. _____

18. _____

19. _____

20. _____

Home Activity Your child wrote list words containing many syllables. Have your child draw a line between syllables. Use a dictionary to help you.

Name _____

Multisyllabic Words

Proofread an Article Circle six spelling errors. Write the words correctly.
Find one capitalization error and write the sentence correctly.

Spelling Words

elementary
vehicle
miniature
probability
opportunity
substitute
variety
literature
elevator
Pennsylvania

ravioli
cafeteria
mosaic
tuxedo
meteorite
fascination
cylinder
intermediate
centennial
curiosity

Fictional Detectives

Literture has its share of famous detectives. writers
have created an enormous variaty of detectives. All have
curiousity about and a fasination with crime. Usually, they
are average people with an especially high probility of
being right in the middle of a crime scene! As one famous
detective said, "It's elamentry, my dear Watson!"

1. _____   2. _____

3. _____   4. _____

5. _____   6. _____

7. _____

_____

Proofread Words Circle the word that is spelled correctly.

8. A _____ looks like a rock.

   metorit   meteoright   meteorite

9. I made a _____ out of glass tile.

   mosaic   mosesic   mosiac

10. My 99-year-old grandfather will have his _____ birthday next year.

    centenial   centennial   cintennial

11. William Penn was the founder of _____.

    Pennsylvania   Pennysylvania   Pennysalvenia

12. The tour _____ can go on land and water.

    veacle   vehicle   vehical

13. A soup can is a _____.

    cylindar   cylander   cylinder

14. My dog is a _____ poodle.

    miniature   miniture   miniatur

Frequently Misspelled Words

usually
especially

Home Activity Your child identified misspelled multisyllabic words. Ask your child to select four list words and tell you how many syllables are in each word.

62

Spelling Words

Spelling Words				
music	musician	select	selection	sign
signal	part	partial	haste	hasten
protect	protection	magic	magician	resign
resignation	electric	electrician	condemn	condemnation

Words in Context Complete each sentence with a list word.

1. John was forced to ____ as the class president.   1. _____

2. The string trio was missing one ____.   2. _____

3. She had a look of ____ on her face.   3. _____

4. A(n) ____ works with electricity.   4. _____

5. The ____ pulled a rabbit out of a hat.   5. _____

6. We need a piano for ____ class.   6. _____

7. The crowd's noises are a ____ of discontent.   7. _____

8. She left in ____ and lost her shoe.   8. _____

9. Mom said the ____ bill was due today.   9. _____

10. The clown performed a few ____ tricks.   10. _____

Antonyms Write the list word that has the opposite or nearly opposite meaning.

11. whole   11. _____

12. do not choose   12. _____

13. harm   13. _____

14. recommendation   14. _____

15. delay   15. _____

Synonyms Write the list word that has the same or nearly the same meaning.

16. incomplete   16. _____

17. indicator   17. _____

18. security   18. _____

19. choice   19. _____

20. denounce   20. _____

Home Activity Your child wrote related words. Have your child tell you a synonym or an antonym for a list word.

Name _____

Related Words

Proofread an E-Mail Shawnelle wrote an e-mail to her friend. Circle six spelling errors and one capitalization error. Write the corrections on the lines.

> Dear nancy,
>
> I had a great time at the outdoor musick festival. The hole group played so well. I especially liked the selecshun played by the alectric guitars. Playing without a conductor must be hard. It was difficult to see who gave the signle to start. When it began raining I wondered what they would do to protek the instruments. Luckily I had a raincoat which kept me dry! Thanks again for giving me your extra ticket.
>
> Your friend,
>
> Kim

Spelling Words

music
musician
select
selection
sign
signal
part
partial
haste
hasten

protect
protection
magic
magician
resign
resignation
electric
electrician
condemn
condemnation

1. _____   2. _____
3. _____   4. _____
5. _____   6. _____
7. _____

Proofread Words Circle the correct spelling of the word.

8. musishun   musician   musicshun

9. magisshun   magicshun   magician

10. partial   partshel   parshel

11. select   selekt   selek

12. haston   hastin   hasten

13. resignashun   resinashun   resignation

14. finaly   finally   finely

15. electrician   electreshun   aletrician

16. condemnation   condemmation   condennation

Frequently Misspelled Words

finally
whole
want

Home Activity Your child identified misspelled words in a paragraph. Ask your child to name a pair of list words and describe how one of the consonants is pronounced differently in each.

Name _____

Greek Word Parts

Spelling Words				
artist	tourism	biology	phobia	heroism
geology	cartoonist	technology	journalism	hydrophobia
violinist	ecology	patriotism	vocalist	meteorology
zoology	claustrophobia	capitalism	novelist	technophobia

Classifying Write the list word that best fits each group.

1. animal, study, science, ____   1. _____

2. travel, pleasure, recreation, ____   2. _____

3. soprano, bass, tenor, ____   3. _____

4. paint, canvas, sculpture, ____   4. _____

5. rocks, minerals, earth, ____   5. _____

6. plants, animals, study, ____   6. _____

7. courage, bravery, fortitude, ____   7. _____

8. weather, forecast, barometer, ____   8. _____

9. writing, reporting, news, ____   9. _____

10. fear, water, abnormal, ____   10. _____

Definitions

11. a persistent, abnormal fear or dislike   11. _____

12. one who draws a comic strip   12. _____

13. a person who writes novels   13. _____

14. the development of new ways to solve problems   14. _____

15. an abnormal fear of technology   15. _____

16. a person who plays the violin   16. _____

17. love and devotion to one's country   17. _____

18. economic system based on the private ownership of industry   18. _____

19. fear of being in small or enclosed spaces   19. _____

20. study of the relation of living things to their
environment and one another   20. _____

Home Activity Your child wrote words that have Greek word parts. Have your child underline the Greek word part in each word.

Greek Word Parts

Proofread an Article Circle six spelling errors in the article. Write the corrections on the lines. Find the sentence with two punctuation errors and write the sentence correctly.

Vacation in Millville

This year many of Millville's families will spend their summer vacations at home. The city's bureau of torism has great ideas on where to go and what to see. The Museum of Natural History has exhibits on geology and metorology. Meanwhile Millville's war memorial holds stories of local herosm and patritism Kids of all ages are invited to the park's month-long festival of ecology and zology. With all that Millville has to offer, its bound to be a fun summer!

1. _____   2. _____

3. _____   4. _____

5. _____   6. _____

7. _____

_____

Proofread Words Circle the correct spelling of the word.

8. journlism   journalism   jurnalism

9. violinist   vilinist   vylinist

10. captalism   capitalism   capetlism

11. tecknology   teknology   technology

12. cartoonist   cartunist   cartoonis

13. eclogy   ekology   ecology

14. biology   bilogy   biologie

15. clastrofobia   claustraphobia   claustrophobia

16. hidrofobia   hydrophobia   hydrofobia

Home Activity Your child identified misspelled list words. Ask your child to spell four words, each with a different Greek word part, and tell you what the words mean.

Latin Roots

Spelling Words				
describe	interruption	inspection	scribble	respectful
bankrupt	project	injection	manuscript	suspect
subscription	spectacular	eruption	eject	abruptly
prescribe	reject	aspect	rupture	inscribe

Words in Context Write the list words that complete each sentence.

She paged through the mystery **(1)**____ and became convinced that the **(2)**____ was guilty.

1. _____   2. _____

She needed to give it a close **(3)**____ before she announced that she would **(4)**____ it.

3. _____   4. _____

It was a long-term **(5)**____ and would look bad if it ended **(6)**____.

5. _____   6. _____

She had to **(7)**____ in detail any pause or **(8)**____ that occurred.

7. _____   8. _____

Even when the company lost money and went **(9)**____, she remained **(10)**____.

9. _____   10. _____

Word Definitions Write the list word that has the same meaning.

11. purchase of a series of things   11. _____

12. a burst, split, or break   12. _____

13. write carelessly   13. _____

14. an element to be considered   14. _____

15. a way of administering a substance, such as a drug   15. _____

16. an order, set down as a rule or guide   16. _____

17. carve into a material   17. _____

18. put out from a place   18. _____

Home Activity Your child wrote words that have Latin roots. Have your child tell you five list words and identify the Latin root in each word. Have your child spell each word.

Name _____

Latin Roots

Proofread an Article Circle six spelling errors in the article. Write the words correctly. Find a punctuation error and write the sentence correctly.

Spelling Words

describe
interruption
inspection
scribble
respectful
bankrupt
project
injection
manuscript
suspect

subscription
spectacular
eruption
eject
abruptly
prescribe
reject
aspect
rupture
inscribe

Library News

Police spent all morning in the ancient manuscript department of our library. They left about an hour later, shaking their heads, barely able to discribe what happened. During the morning inspection, I found the suspect about to scribbel his name apon the cover of a rare manuscript. I gasped. Surprised by the interuption the suspect turned abruptly. I grabbed him by the collar and proceeded to eject him from the premises. During police questioning, the suspect revealed his plans for a spectacilar project. He intended to enscribe his name on all 600 volumes of ancient and rare manuscripts. Luckily, I was able to stop that from happening.

1. _____   2. _____

3. _____   4. _____

5. _____   6. _____

7. _____

_____

Frequently Misspelled Words

into
upon

Proofread Words Circle the correct spelling of each word.

8. bankupt   bankrupt   bankrup

9. injection   enjection   injekshun

10. aruption   erubtion   eruption

11. respectfull   respectful   rispectful

12. prescribe   preescribe   preskribe

13. subsription   subscription   subscreption

14. rejekt   reject   reject

15. rupshure   repture   rupture

16. aspect   espekt   aspict

Home Activity Your child identified misspelled list words. Ask your child to say five list words, tell the Latin root for each, and then spell and define each word.

68

Name _____

Greek Word Parts

Spelling Words				
telephone	graphic	thermometer	photographer	centimeter
paragraph	telescope	diameter	photocopy	speedometer
telegraph	millimeter	autograph	television	barometer
telecommute	pedometer	phonograph	kilometer	telephoto

Classifying Write the list word that best fits each group.

1. circle, radius, circumference, _____

2. microscope, binoculars, _____

3. letters, words, sentences, _____

4. tape cassette, compact disc, mp3 player, _____

5. air pressure, weather, instrument, _____

6. instrument, measure, speed, _____

7. communicate, wire, electric, _____

8. call, dial, talk, _____

9. camera, pictures, person, _____

10. mile, furlong, fathom, _____

Definitions Write the list word that has the same meaning.

11. one hundredth of a meter

12. a person's own signature

13. a photographic copy of written or printed work

14. instrument for measuring temperature

15. electronic device that shows images on a screen

16. instrument for measuring distance walked

17. one thousandth of a meter

18. to work at a location remote from one's place of employment, making use of a computer

19. a lens that makes distant objects appear magnified

20. a picture, design, or visual display

11. _____

12. _____

13. _____

14. _____

15. _____

16. _____

17. _____

18. _____

19. _____

20. _____

School + Home **Home Activity** Your child wrote related words that are spelled similarly but pronounced differently. Say list words and have your child say and spell the list word that is related.

Name _____

Greek Word Parts

Proofread an Article Circle six spelling errors in the article. Write the words correctly. Find a punctuation error and write the sentence correctly.

From Feet to Kilometers

Each time your feet hit the pavement, your body vibrates. A pedimeter senses these vibrations and moves a counter forward, counting the total number of steps. Then it's computer changes the number of steps into miles or meters. A bicycle odometer does something similar. It counts the number of times a wheel goes around. A computer uses the dimeter of the wheel to compute the distance traveled, changing centameters to meters. Rather than counting wheel revolutions, automobile odometers count the number of turns made by the car's transmission gears. A computer changes the milimeters the gears move to the kilometers the automobile moves. Can you guess how a speedameter works.

Spelling Words

telephone
graphic
thermometer
photographer
centimeter
paragraph
telescope
diameter
photocopy
speedometer

telegraph
millimeter
autograph
television
barometer
telecommute
pedometer
phonograph
kilometer
telephoto

1. _____   2. _____

3. _____   4. _____

5. _____   6. _____

7. _____

_____

Frequently Misspelled Words

I'm
it's
let's

Proofread Words Circle the correct spelling of each word.

8. telecomute   telacommute   telecommute

9. photacopy   photocopy   photocoppy

10. telescope   telascope   teliscope

11. grafic   graphik   graphic

12. thermameter   thermometer   thermemeter

13. photographer   photagrapher   photographor

14. barameter   barimeter   barometer

Home Activity Your child identified misspelled words. Ask your child to spell four words, each with a different Greek word part, and tell you what the words mean.

Multisyllabic Words

Spelling Words

elementary	opportunity	elevator	mosaic	cylinder
vehicle	substitute	Pennsylvania	tuxedo	intermediate
miniature	variety	ravioli	meteorite	centennial
probability	literature	cafeteria	fascination	curiosity

Analogies Write the list word that completes each comparison.

1. Store is to shop as lunchroom is to _____.

2. Poodle is to dog as poem is to _____.

3. Building block is to cube as tin can is to _____.

4. Huge is to giant as tiny is to _____.

5. Chicago is to Illinois as Philadelphia is to _____.

6. Silk is to fabric as car is to _____.

7. Apple is to fruit as _____ is to pasta.

8. Pleasant is to nice as basic is to _____.

9. Casual is to jeans as formal is to _____.

10. Beginning is to elementary as middle is to _____.

Alphabetize Write the ten list words below in alphabetical order.

meteorite	elevator
curiosity	opportunity
probability	substitute
fascination	centennial
mosaic	variety

11. _____

12. _____

13. _____

14. _____

15. _____

16. _____

17. _____

18. _____

19. _____

20. _____

 Home Activity Your child has completed analogies for multisyllabic words. Take turns making up analogies for list words and completing them.

Name _____

Related Words

Analogies Write the word that completes each sentence.

1. Pieces are to puzzle as notes are to _____.

2. Postpone is to delay as speed up is to _____.

3. Pipes are to plumber as lights are to _____.

4. Complete is to undone as whole is to _____.

5. Food is to nourishment as defense is to _____.

6. Sign up is to enroll as drop out is to _____.

7. Approve is to disapprove as praise is to _____.

8. Route is to path as choice is to _____.

9. Smart is to intelligent as symbol is to _____.

10. Drill is to carpenter as wand is to _____.

Word Clues Write the list word that fits each clue.

11. a strong statement of disapproval   _____

12. a person who plays music   _____

13. to choose   _____

14. a portion   _____

15. tricks and illusions   _____

16. an action or gesture to communicate   _____

17. great speed   _____

18. watch over   _____

19. full of electricity   _____

20. a formal letter that you're leaving   _____

Copyright © Savvas Learning Company LLC. All Rights Reserved.

72

Name _____

Greek Word Parts

Spelling Words				
artist	tourism	biology	phobia	heroism
geology	cartoonist	technology	journalism	hydrophobia
violinist	ecology	patriotism	vocalist	meteorology
zoology	claustrophobia	capitalism	novelist	technophobia

Words in Context Write the list words that complete each sentence.

The School of the Arts is the best if you want to be an **(1)** _____ and paint or a **(2)** _____ and write.

1. _____   2. _____

The soldiers in the platoon showed great courage, **(3)** _____, and **(4)** _____.

3. _____   4. _____

Rafael studies environmental science, or **(5)** _____; he wants to use engineering science, or **(6)** _____, to improve the environment.

5. _____   6. _____

The **(7)** _____ titled his humorous drawing about the market economy, "**(8)** _____ at Work."

7. _____   8. _____

The **(9)** _____ students presented a news program about **(10)** _____, the fear of small, enclosed spaces.

9. _____   10. _____

Azir studied all living things, or **(11)** _____, before he decided to major in **(12)** _____, the study of animals.

11. _____   12. _____

Earth science courses include **(13)** _____, the study of rocks, and **(14)** _____ the study of weather and climate.

13. _____   14. _____

Synonyms Write the list word that has the same, or nearly the same, meaning.

15. violin player _____   16. recreational travel _____

17. singer _____   18. fear of technology _____

19. strong fear _____   20. fear of water _____

Home Activity Your child has learned to spell words with Greek word parts. Ask your child to organize the list words into groups according to word parts and tell what each word part means.

Name _____

Latin Roots

Classifying Write the list word that belongs in each group.

1. book, pamphlet, brochure, _____

2. shot, vaccine, inoculation, _____

3. draw, write, doodle, _____

4. write, etch, chisel, _____

5. tear, void, break, _____

6. break, gap, discontinuity, _____

7. ejection, geyser, outburst, _____

8. appearance, part, perspective, _____

9. review, survey, examination, _____

10. magazines, monthly, newspapers, _____

Synonyms Write the list word that has the same, or nearly the same, meaning.

11. turn down   _____

12. distrust   _____

13. suddenly   _____

14. broke   _____

15. dictate   _____

16. task   _____

17. throw out   _____

18. tell details   _____

19. courteous   _____

20. wonderful   _____

Home Activity Your child has learned to spell words with Latin roots. Take turns brainstorming a word that has one of the list word roots. Look up each word in the dictionary to confirm it comes from a Latin word.

Name _____

Greek Word Parts

Words in Context Write the list words that complete each sentence.

A **(1)** _____ lens magnifies distant objects; a **(2)** _____ also magnifies distant objects.

1. _____   2. _____

A **(3)** _____ keeps track of the distance walked; a **(4)** _____ keeps track of a vehicle's speed.

3. _____   4. _____

A **(5)** _____ and a land line **(6)** _____ both carry communication over wires.

5. _____   6. _____

A **(7)** _____ and a **(8)** _____ are each smaller than an inch.

7. _____   8. _____

You can use a **(9)** _____ and a **(10)** _____ to learn about the weather.

9. _____   10. _____

Word Definitions Write the list word that matches the definition.

11. a group of sentences developing a single idea   11. _____

12. record player   12. _____

13. picture or other visual representation   13. _____

14. a copy made with a photocopier   14. _____

15. twice the length of a circle's radius   15. _____

16. a person's own signature   16. _____

17. one thousand meters   17. _____

18. person who takes photographs   18. _____

19. work from home using computers, and other electronic devices   19. _____

20. a device that shows images on a screen   20. _____

Home Activity Your child has learned to spell words with Greek word parts. Ask your child to organize the list words into groups according to word parts and tell what each word part means.

Name _____

Suffixes *-ous, -sion, -ion, -ation*

Spelling Words				
famous	invention	election	furious	imagination
education	nervous	explanation	various	decision
relaxation	conversation	tension	humorous	exhibition
attraction	invasion	creation	occupation	destination

Synonyms Write the list word that has the same or almost the same meaning as the underlined word or phrase.

1. We will reach our <u>journey's end</u> after four days of traveling.

2. People who are <u>well known</u> are often stopped by fans on the street.

3. Sometimes it's very hard to make a <u>choice</u>.

4. I had a very long <u>talk</u> on the phone with my cousin.

5. The 5th graders had a special <u>art show</u> in the auditorium.

6. I felt <u>worried</u> and had butterflies in my stomach.

7. The army ants launched an <u>attack</u> at our picnic.

8. It takes a lot of <u>creative thoughts</u> to write a story.

9. What was your <u>excuse</u> for being late?

10. Who won that close <u>vote</u> last month?

1. _____

2. _____

3. _____

4. _____

5. _____

6. _____

7. _____

8. _____

9. _____

10. _____

Definitions Write the list word that fits each definition.

11. stretching or a strain

12. a thing that delights

13. something that is created

14. funny and amusing

15. knowledge and skills learned

16. differing from one another

17. condition of being relaxed

18. something made for the first time

19. what someone does to earn a living

20. full of wild, fierce anger

11. _____

12. _____

13. _____

14. _____

15. _____

16. _____

17. _____

18. _____

19. _____

20. _____

Home Activity Your child wrote words that have suffixes. Have your child underline the suffix in each word.

Suffixes *-ous*, *-sion*, *-ion*, *-ation*

Proofread an Essay Circle five spelling errors in the essay. Write the words correctly. Find a sentence with a capitalization error and write the sentence correctly.

Spelling Words
famous
invention
election
furious
imagination
education
nervous
explanation
various
decision
relaxation
conversation
tension
humorous
exhibition
attraction
invasion
creation
occupation
destination

Laughing Helps

When I feel nervos or edgy, I call my friend. Having a friendly conversasion really helps. My friend is truly funny and tells humorus stories. I told my friend that she would be famus one day. She laughed and said, "well, I don't want to be a performer. I have to finish my educasion first." Still, I think being a comedian seems like a great occupation for her.

1. _____   2. _____

3. _____   4. _____

5. _____

6. _____

Proofread Words Circle the word that is spelled correctly. Write the word.

7. varius	varous	various	7. _____
8. invension	invention	invensiun	8. _____
9. tention	tensiun	tension	9. _____
10. furious	furyous	furius	10. _____
11. attration	attraction	attracshun	11. _____
12. destinashun	destinasion	destination	12. _____
13. relacsation	relaxation	relaxasion	13. _____
14. exsibition	exabition	exhibition	14. _____
15. election	elektion	elecsion	15. _____
16. invation	invasion	invashion	16. _____

Frequently Misspelled Words
didn't
said
don't

Home Activity Your child identified misspelled list words. Say a suffix and have your child tell you a list word ending in that suffix. Then have your child spell the word.

Name_____

Final Syllable *-ant, -ent, -ance, -ence*

Antonyms Write the list word that has the opposite or almost the opposite meaning of the underlined word or phrase.

1. I was <u>certain</u> to ask for help on my assignment.

2. We thought his <u>presence</u> was the cause of the loss.

3. We had trouble finding the <u>exit</u> to the building.

4. The facts in the case are <u>unimportant</u>.

5. Our students strive for <u>poor quality</u> in all they do.

6. That constant buzzing in the television is a(n) <u>occasional</u> annoyance.

7. A good employee is hard working and <u>inconsistent</u>.

8. It takes a while to develop self-assurance and <u>shyness</u>.

9. Car exhaust is an air <u>cleaner</u>.

10. By human standards, slugs and snails are not <u>stupid</u>.

1. _____

2. _____

3. _____

4. _____

5. _____

6. _____

7. _____

8. _____

9. _____

10. _____

Definitions Write the list word on the line that has the same meaning.

11. anything that shows what is true and what is not

12. a kind of sale

13. financial protection against harm, illness, or loss

14. vehicle that provides transportation to the hospital

15. a change

16. a person or thing serving as an example

17. knowing little or nothing

18. what is seen, done, or lived through

19. a meeting of interested persons to discuss a particular subject

20. the act of coming into sight

11. _____

12. _____

13. _____

14. _____

15. _____

16. _____

17. _____

18. _____

19. _____

20. _____

Home Activity Your child wrote words that have syllables ending in *-ant, -ent, -ance, -ence*. Have your child underline the final syllable in each word.

Name _____

Final Syllable *-ant, -ent, -ance, -ence*

Proofread an Article Circle and write six spelling errors. Circle one capitalization error and write the sentence correctly.

Help Is on the Way

With sirens wailing, the ambulence driver carefully winds through traffic. It takes a lot of confidents to do this importent job. In large cities, with persistant traffic, a driver must be extra careful. Still, the Driver must take the fastest route to the emergency room. Time makes all the differants when people need emergency care. All drivers try to get each won of their patients to the emergency room entrance as quickly as possible.

1. _____   2. _____

3. _____   4. _____

5. _____   6. _____

7. _____

_____

Proofread Words Circle the correct spelling of the list word. Write the word.

8. absense	abcense	absence	8. _____
9. intelligant	intelligent	intellagent	9. _____
10. insurance	insurants	insurence	10. _____
11. pollutent	pollutant	pollutint	11. _____
12. ignorent	ignorint	ignorant	12. _____
13. apperence	appearance	appearants	13. _____
14. important	importent	inportant	14. _____
15. hezitent	hesitent	hesitant	15. _____

Home Activity Your child identified misspelled list words. Ask your child to name the four words he or she has the most difficulty spelling and spell them for you.

Spelling Words

important
experience
ignorant
entrance
difference
instance
absence
appearance
intelligent
evidence

pollutant
clearance
confidence
conference
insurance
ambulance
hesitant
consistent
excellence
persistent

Frequently Misspelled Words

off
one
tired

Name _____

Latin Roots

Spelling Words				
portable	audience	decade	territory	auditorium
dictionary	terrace	reporter	December	contradict
export	decimal	audit	transport	audition
prediction	import	jurisdiction	decathlon	terrain

Words in Context Write the list words that complete each sentence.

She sang for her **(1)** _____ in the large **(2)** _____.

1. _____   2. _____

Most of the **(3)** _____ was hilly but we found a nice flat **(4)** _____ for a short rest.

3. _____   4. _____

We **(5)** _____ grain to China and **(6)** _____ Chinese toys and clothes.

5. _____   6. _____

The **(7)** _____ took her notes using a **(8)** _____ recorder.

7. _____   8. _____

He was bold enough to insist his definition was right and **(9)** _____ the **(10)** _____.

9. _____   10. _____

Word Definitions Write the list word that has the same meaning.

11. move something

12. a statement made about the future

13. a number written using base ten

14. those who view or listen to a performance

15. land or region

16. a ten-year period

17. examine carefully for accuracy

18. legal power

19. a competition having ten events

20. twelfth month of the year

11. _____

12. _____

13. _____

14. _____

15. _____

16. _____

17. _____

18. _____

19. _____

20. _____

Home Activity Your child wrote words that have Latin roots. Have your child tell you five list words and identify the Latin root in each word. Have your child spell each word.

Name _____

Latin Roots

Proofread an Article Circle six spelling errors in the article. Write the words correctly. Find a punctuation error and write the sentence correctly.

Hard Work

Only a superb athlete can prevail in a decathalon The competition includes five events on each of two days. There is an enthusiastic audience for most events, especially those held in an auditorum. Races may be won by less than a thousandth of a second. However, the jumps, shot put, and javelin events may be won by as much as a decimeter. Reportors find it difficult to make a predikshion regarding a winner because winners are determined by a system which awards decemal values based on performance. Today, only male athletes may enter in too a decathlon. Women athletes compete in a heptathlon, a competition with seven events.

---

1. _____   2. _____

3. _____   4. _____

5. _____   6. _____

7. _____

_____

Proofread Words Circle the correct spelling of each word.

8. esport	axport	export			
9. terace	terrace	terrece	**15.** jursdiction	juresdiction	jurisdiction
10. emport	amport	import	**16.** territory	terratory	terretory
11. decade	decad	deckade	**17.** Dicimber	December	Dacember
12. aduit	audit	audet	**18.** trenspart	trenspert	transport
13. dictionary	dictoinary	dictionery	**19.** contradict	contredict	controdict
14. portabel	portable	portible	**20.** audition	aduition	audetin

Home Activity Your child identified misspelled list words. Ask your child to say five list words, tell the Latin root for each, and then spell and define each word.

Name _____

Related Words

Spelling Words				
clean	cleanse	inspire	inspiration	legal
legality	define	definition	please	pleasant
combine	combination	human	humanity	organ
organist	crime	criminal	recognize	recognition

Words in Context Write the list words that complete the sentence.

I use the **(1)** _____ of other artists to **(2)** _____ me. (inspiration, inspire)

1. _____   2. _____

The **(3)** _____ looked tiny as she stood in front of the **(4)** _____. (organ, organist)

3. _____   4. _____

(5) _____ the eggs and sugar; add the flour and spices to the **(6)** _____. (combine, combination)

5. _____   6. _____

She said, "Jake, **(7)** _____ be **(8)** _____ to your Aunt Martha." (please, pleasant)

7. _____   8. _____

"I'm not a **(9)** _____," he said. "I didn't commit the **(10)** _____." (crime, criminal)

9. _____   10. _____

Definitions Write the list word that has the same meaning as the word or phrase.

11. dirt free _____   12. wash _____

13. word's meaning _____   14. person _____

15. identify something _____   16. specify meaning _____

17. lawfulness _____   18. allowed by law _____

19. appreciation, fame _____   20. quality of being human _____

School + Home **Home Activity** Your child wrote related words that are spelled similarly but pronounced differently. Say list words and have your child say and spell the list word that is related.

Name _____

Related Words

Proofread an Article Circle six spelling errors and one sentence containing punctuation errors. Write the corrections on the lines.

Spelling Words

clean
cleanse
inspire
inspiration
legal
legality
define
definition
please
pleasant

combine
combination
human
humanity
organ
organist
crime
criminal
recognize
recognition

Courts

The United States Supreme Court is the highest court in the land. Often it is asked to determine the legalaty of a law. The Supreme Court has the right to either reconize or deny any appeal submitted to it. Some times it difines conditions under which an existing law may be leagle or illegal. The Constitution and laws of each state establish the state courts. These state courts handle criminul cases. States also usually have courts that handle specific legal matters. These include juvenile court; family court; and others.

1. _____ 2. _____

3. _____ 4. _____

5. _____ 6. _____

7. _____

_____

Proofread Words Circle the correct spelling of the word.

8. crim   crieme   crime

9. recognition   raconition   reconition

10. plese   please   pleeze

11. orgunist   organist   orgenist

12. humen   homan   human

13. enspire   inspire   inspir

14. orgun   argon   organ

15. humanity   humenety   humenity

16. combination   comination   cumination

Home Activity Your child identified misspelled words. Write the first four letters of a list word and have your child write the two related words.

Name _____

Easily Confused Words

Spelling Words				
quiet	quite	finely	finally	except
accept	than	then	since	sense
affect	effect	from	form	later
latter	adapt	adopt	medal	metal

Definitions Write the list word that means the same as each word or phrase.

1. silent

2. at last

3. receive

4. shape

5. a type of award

1. _____

2. _____

3. _____

4. _____

5. _____

Words in Context Write a list word to finish each sentence.

6. How will this score ___ my grade?

7. I'll see you ___.

8. They plan to ___ a child soon.

9. By ___ we should know the results of the race.

10. My aunt has a good ___ of humor.

11. I think this project is not ___ finished yet.

12. This piano has been very ___ tuned.

13. Everyone was there ___ me.

14. I would rather go to a movie ___ do my homework.

15. I haven't seen her ___ last year.

16. What ___ will this poor test score have on my overall grade?

17. I like to walk home ___ school.

18. I prefer the former choice to the ___.

19. It is important to be able to ___ to new situations.

20. The magnet picked up the ___ pieces.

6. _____

7. _____

8. _____

9. _____

10. _____

11. _____

12. _____

13. _____

14. _____

15. _____

16. _____

17. _____

18. _____

19. _____

20. _____

Home Activity Your child matched words with definitions and finished sentences. Ask your child to define the word *adapt*.

84

Name _____

Easily Confused Words

Proofread a Dialogue Circle six spelling mistakes in the article below.
Write them correctly. Find a sentence with a misplaced comma. Write the
sentence correctly.

My Brother the Hero

When my brother finely got back form serving
overseas, my family was happy and proud. We
attended a ceremony where we watched him
except a metal. When he stood up to receive
his award, we were very quite. Latter we went
out to dinner to celebrate his return.

---

1. _____   2. _____

3. _____   4. _____

5. _____   6. _____

7. _____

_____

Proofread Words Circle the word that is spelled correctly.
Write it on the line.

8. axcept	accept	8.	_____
9. adupt	adapt	9.	_____
10. adoped	adopt	10.	_____
11. affect	afect	11.	_____
12. except	exsept	12.	_____
13. finaly	finally	13.	_____
14. sense	sence	14.	_____
15. then	thun	15.	_____

Spelling Words

quiet
quite
finely
finally
except
accept
than
then
since
sense

affect
effect
from
form
later
latter
adapt
adopt
medal
metal

Frequently Misspelled Words

where
were

Home Activity Your child identified misspelled words. Ask your child to pick a list word and
use it in a sentence.

Name _____

Suffixes -ous, -sion, -ion, -ation

Spelling Words				
famous	imagination	various	tension	invasion
invention	education	decision	humorous	creation
election	nervous	relaxation	exhibition	occupation
furious	explanation	conversation	attraction	destination

Antonyms Write the list word that has the opposite or nearly the opposite meaning.

1. serious _____

2. relaxed _____

3. repulsion _____

4. unknown _____

5. destruction _____

6. calm _____

7. uncertainty _____

8. alike _____

Words in Context Complete each sentence with a list word.

9. Reading, writing, and math are important parts of your _____.

10. The lightbulb was a marvelous _____.

11. Nursing is a helpful _____.

12. In a good _____, everyone has a chance to speak.

13. We saw a(n) _____ of modern art at the museum.

14. Some people play card games for _____.

15. The beach is a popular summer _____.

16. Our picnic was ruined by a(n) _____ of ants.

17. You must use your _____ to write a compelling poem.

18. It is important for citizens to vote in each _____.

19. Stretching a rubber band increases its _____.

20. You must have a good _____ for missing soccer practice.

Home Activity Your child has been learning to spell words with suffixes. Call out some of the list words and ask your child to give a synonym or antonym for each word.

Name _____

Final Syllable *-ant*, *-ent*, *-ance*, *-ence*

Analogies Write the word that completes each comparison.

1. Happiness is to sadness as presence is to _____.

2. Sweet is to sour as educated is to _____.

3. Rose is to flower as smoke is to _____.

4. Trip is to journey as example is to _____.

5. Night is to day as exit is to _____.

6. Pretty is to lovely as smart is to _____.

7. Doctor is to hospital as paramedic is to _____.

8. Heat is to cold as sameness is to _____.

9. Game is to sport as meeting is to _____.

10. Difficult is to easy as insignificant is to _____.

Words in Context Complete each sentence with a list word.

11. The car repairs were paid for by the _____ company.

12. The jury considered the _____ against the man on trial.

13. Bright autumn colors gave the trees a lovely _____.

14. The soccer players liked the referee because his calls were _____.

15. Confronting a bear must be a frightening _____.

16. Because he was shy, Will was _____ to meet people.

17. There was a(n) _____ sale of snow boots at the end of the winter.

18. That baseball player has much _____ in his ability.

19. At the spring assembly, the best students were rewarded for _____.

20. To succeed in your goal, you must be _____.

Home Activity Your child learned to spell words with the final syllables *-ant*, *-ent*, *-ance*, and *-ence*. Ask your child to find an example of a word with each ending in a magazine and then spell each word without looking at the magazine.

Name _____

Latin Roots

Spelling Words				
portable	audience	decade	territory	auditorium
dictionary	terrace	reporter	December	contradict
export	decimal	audit	transport	audition
prediction	import	jurisdiction	decathlon	terrain

Classifying Write the list word that belongs in each group.

1. state, country, region, _____

2. patio, deck, balcony, _____

3. September, October, November, _____

4. week, month, year, _____

5. races, hurdle, shot put, _____

6. aquarium, solarium, gymnasium, _____

7. writer, investigator, researcher, _____

8. integer, fraction, whole number, _____

9. thesaurus, encyclopedia, handbook, _____

10. court, claims, civil, _____

Synonyms Write the list word that has the same or nearly the same meaning.

11. tryout   _____

12. forecast   _____

13. ground   _____

14. onlookers   _____

15. move   _____

16. check   _____

17. send   _____

18. dispute   _____

19. moveable   _____

20. bring in   _____

Home Activity Your child has learned to spell words with Latin roots. Take turns brainstorming a word that has one of the list word roots. Look up each word in the dictionary to confirm that it comes from a Latin word.

Name _____

Related Words

Spelling Words				
clean	inspire	legal	define	please
cleanse	inspiration	legality	definition	pleasant
combine	human	organ	crime	recognize
combination	humanity	organist	criminal	recognition

Analogies Write the word that completes each sentence.

1. Pepper is to salt as dirty is to _____.

2. Beast is to animal as person is to _____.

3. Stop is to go as separate is to _____.

4. Violin is to violinist as organ is to _____.

5. Good-bye is to hello as thank you is to _____.

6. Exhilaration is to excitement as encouragement is to _____.

7. Individual is to single as mixture is to _____.

8. Tool is to hammer as instrument is to _____.

9. Earth is to world as mankind is to _____.

10. Unwind is to relax as unlawful is to _____.

Synonyms Write the list word that has the same or nearly the same meaning.

11. wash _____

12. lawful _____

13. meaning _____

14. agreeable _____

15. acknowledgement _____

Antonyms Write the list word that has the opposite or nearly the opposite meaning.

16. not notice _____

17. discourage _____

18. confuse _____

19. unlawfulness _____

20. legal _____

Home Activity Your child has learned to spell related words. Read several pairs of words from the list. Ask your child to explain how knowing the spelling of one word in the pair can help in spelling the other word.

Easily Confused Words

Spelling Words				
quiet	except	since	from	adapt
quite	accept	sense	form	adopt
finely	than	affect	later	medal
finally	then	effect	latter	metal

Antonyms Write the list word that has the opposite or nearly the opposite meaning.

1. coarsely _____

2. reject _____

3. earlier _____

4. noisy _____

5. now _____

Synonyms Write the list word that has the same or nearly the same meaning.

6. result _____

7. reward _____

8. very _____

9. because _____

10. select _____

Analogies Write the word that completes each comparison.

11. First is to last as former is to _____.

12. Start is to begin as at last is to _____.

13. In is to out as to is to _____.

14. Milk is to drink as iron is to _____.

15. Buy is to purchase as influence is to _____.

16. North is to direction as sight is to _____.

17. Also is to too as but is to _____.

18. Gift is to present as shape is to _____.

19. Work is to labor as change is to _____.

20. Log is to dog as fan is to _____.

Home Activity Your child has learned to spell sound-alike words. Ask your child to name three pairs of list words, spell each word, and explain how they differ in meaning.